Canal Cruising in France
A Guide for Rental Boaters

Michael Walsh

Other recent books by Michael Walsh

Sequitur - To Cape Horn in Comfort and Style
Published 2013 - ISBN: 978-09919556-0-2

Carefree on the European Canals
Published 2014 - ISBN: 978-09919556-4-0

Through 1001 French Locks
Published 2015 - ISBN: 978-09919556-7-1

Canal Cruising in France
A Guide for Rental Boaters

Copyright © 2015 by Michael Walsh

Cover by Edith Gelin & Michael Walsh

All rights reserved. No part of this book may be reproduced in any form by any electronic or mechanical means, including photocopying, scanning, recording, or information storage and retrieval without permission in writing from the author.

ISBN: 978-09919556-9-5

Published by Zonder Zorg Press

www.zonderzorg.ca
michael@zonderzorg.ca

Printed in the United States of America
on Sustainable Forestry Initiative® (SFI®) Certified Sourcing papers

Table of Contents

	Acknowledgements	vi
	Introduction	vii
1.	Setting the Scene	1
2.	The Regions of France	9
3.	Historic French Barges	45
4.	Historic Dutch Barges	51
5.	Pleasure Cruising in France	54
6.	A Look at the Rental Boats	58
7.	A Look at the Locks	68
8.	Basic Boat Handling	79
9.	Line Handling and Safety in Locks	87
10.	Rules of the Road and CEVNI	91
11.	Lock Etiquette and Food for Thought	95
	Glossary of English and French Canal Terms	98

Acknowledgements

Most of the photos in this book were shot by the author and his mate Edi Gelin. Many of the maps in the book were prepared by the author using NASA satellite images. Older maps and images were found in the public domain. The author is grateful for the following: The maps on pages 1 and 2 are from the Voies Navigables de France (VNF) website. The map on page 6 is adapted from one on Wikimedia Commons by Thomas Steiner. The maps on pages 9, 10, 13, 14, 16, 17, 23, 24, 30, 39, 41 and 43 are adapted from ones on Wikimedia Commons. The photos on page 15 are by Benutzer:Reinhard Kraasch and Calips on Wikimedia Commons. The photo at the bottom of page 22 is by JP Tupin on Wikimedia Commons. The photo at the top of page 23 is from the comité régional du tourisme de Franche-Comté. The map and diagram on page 25 are by Pinpin on Wikimedia Commons. The photo at the top of page 37 is by Accrochoc on Wikimedia Commons. The photo at the bottom of page 37 is from the Niclos website. The photo of Saint-Cyrc-Lapopie on page 38 is by Adam Baker on Wikimedia Commons. The photo on page 39 is by JLPC on Wikimedia Commons. The map on page 39 is by Bilz0r on Wikimedia Commons. The photo of Jarnac on page 40 is by JarnaQuais on Wikimedia Commons. The photo of Angoulêm on page 40 is by Thibautsl on Wikimedia Commons. The photo of Dinan on page 42 is by Tango7174 on Wikimedia Commons. The photo of the wine on page 43 is by Jameson Fink on Wikimedia Commons. The photo of Château Plessis-Bourré on page 43 is by Hvane on Wikimedia Commons. Photos of the model and drawing on page 52 were shot by the author of displays in the Fries Scheepvaart Museum, Sneek. The photo of the luxemotor on page 53 is from a model in the Scheepvaartmuseum, Amsterdam. The chart on page 55 is from the VNF website. The photos of the Linssens on page 55 are from the Linssen website. The photos on pages 59 and 60 are from the LeBoat website. The photos on pages 61 and 62 are from the Canalous website. The photos on pages 63 and 64 are from the Nicols website. The photos on pages 65 and 66 are from the Locaboat website. The illustration on Page 69 is adapted from one by Cmglee on Wikimedia Commons. Rights to reproduce the cartoon on page 88 were purchased from vitalimagery.com.

Introduction

Throughout France is a vast network of canals and navigable rivers that lead through a wondrous variety of pastoral settings, medieval towns and villages and vibrant cities. Along the way are vestiges of human habitation spanning the millennia from palaeolithic times onward through a complex history of settlement. The occupation and taming of the land followed the courses of the rivers and across the low passes that link them to each other. The rivers were gradually tamed, canals were built and commerce along them thrived. The coming of rail and then motorized road transportation brought a rapid decline in the commercial use of the canals and by the middle of the twentieth century, many had been abandoned. During the past few decades, the rise of interest in the pleasure use of the historic waterways has led to their restoration.

This book is written to introduce people to navigating, exploring and enjoying the network of French inland waterways. It begins with an outline of the geography and history of inland navigation, starting with a broad view and then narrowing to focus on the rivers and canals of France. An overview of the cruising regions gives a flavour of what to expect in each. There is a look at the variety of boats and barges that historically used the French canals and rivers and at those that still do, including a cross-section of the rental boats that are currently offered by the major companies.

In essence, the book includes the current basic information that is needed to select a French cruising region, choose a rental company and gain an understanding of the styles of boats that are available. There is information on the types of locks and their workings, as well as tips on boat handling, line handling and safety that will allow you to confidently head out cruising on the French canals.

Michael Walsh
Auxonne, France
March 2015

Dedication

This book is for the knowledgeable and skilled operators of commercial barges, pleasure barges and private cruisers on the French canals, all of whom wish for more knowledge and skill among the rental boaters.

Chapter One

Setting the Scene

Across Europe there is a complex network of waterways. The ocean and seas surrounding the continent are interconnected by a web of canals linking watersheds to each other, enabling navigation far inland. There are hundreds of canals making it possible to cross Europe by boat from the North Sea to the Mediterranean, from the Irish Sea to the Black Sea, from the Mediterranean to the Atlantic.

In 1992 continental Europe adopted a classification system for its inland waterways. This was created by the European Council of Ministers of Transport, which rated the canals ECMT Class I to Class VII. The classification was based on the dimensions of the waterway structures, such as lengths and widths of locks, clearance under bridges and the available depths. At the smallest end of the scale, Class I corresponds to the historical Freycinet gauge of France dating to 1879. At the upper end, the larger river classification sizes focus on a waterway's ability to handle mulit-barge convoys propelled by pusher tugs.

Canal Cruising in France

In France today there are ninety-four navigable rivers and canals with a total length of 8800 kilometres and 2165 locks. Most of these waterways are interconnected in the northeastern and the southwestern parts of the country and the remaining 500 kilometres are isolated waterways in western France. About twenty percent of the French waterways are Class IV and above, mainly the major rivers. Of the remainder, the vast majority are Class I and lower with minimal commercial traffic and ideally suited to pleasure cruising.

More than three-quarters of the French inland waterways network is under the jurisdiction of Voies Navigables de France, commonly referred to as the VNF, which was established in 1991 to replace l'Office national de la navigation. Their mandate includes maintaining and operating their portion of the waterways and the environment bordering them.

Setting the Scene

As commercial freight traffic declined along the waterways after the Second World War, there was a slow increase in the number of pleasure boat users. Accelerating this increase through the 1970s and 80s was the rapid rise in the popularity of rental boats. Their growth reached a plateau in the late 1990s and their numbers have declined around thirty percent over the past decade and a half. Meanwhile, the number of private pleasure craft continues to slowly increase, making the current pace on the French canals more peaceful than at any time since the mid 1980s.

To further set the scene, it is necessary to look at the various types of inland waterway. The most fundamental is the tidal river, such as the Garonne, which from its mouth below Bordeaux, is navigable upstream for 90 kilometres, or the tidal Seine, which is a major transportation route allowing seagoing vessels to navigate 124 kilometres upstream toward Paris from the English Channel at Le Havre. On both of these rivers the tidal currents are very strong, so close attention must be paid to the tides, ensuring that the passage is coordinated with favourable currents.

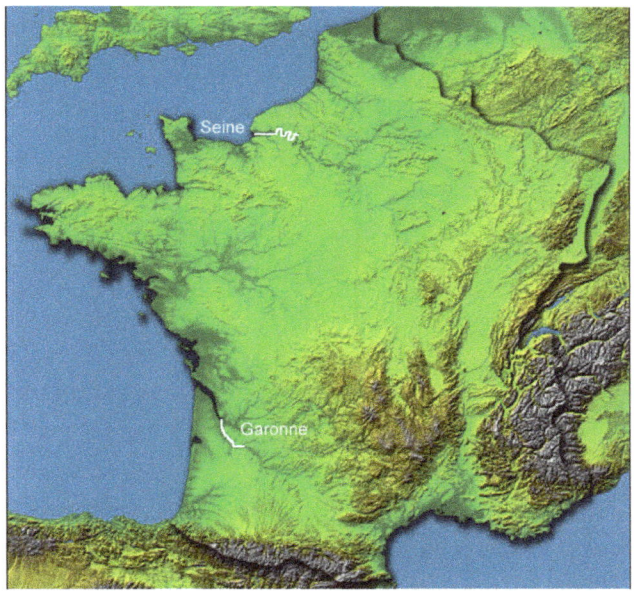

A second type of waterway follows along a non-tidal river that has been tamed and controlled by locks. These locks step the traffic up or down past cataracts or rapids in the river and offer relatively still water in the pounds between successive locks. The locks are often located on a short canal bypassing the dam or weir that is built across the river to maintain the water level upstream. The Rhône and the Saône are good examples of larger lock-controlled rivers. The Rhône takes traffic from the Mediterranean 310 kilometres northward through twelve locks to Lyon. From Lyon, navigation on the Saône continues for another 407 kilometres through twenty-four locks to Corre. On a much smaller scale are the rivers Lot and Baïse in the southwest.

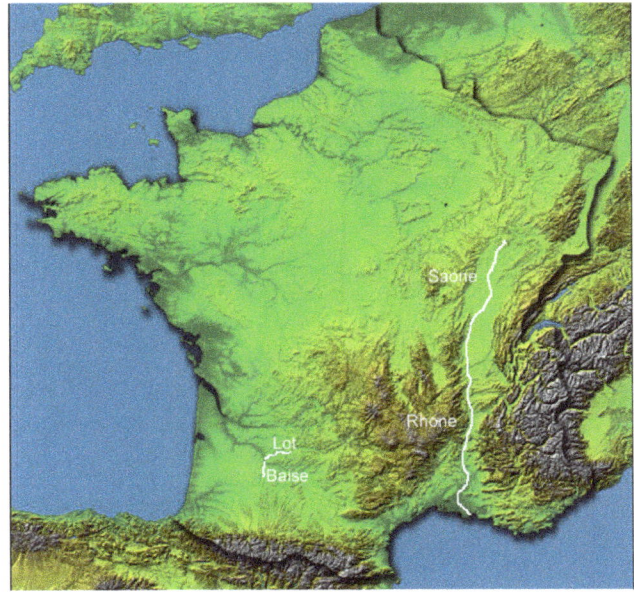

Canal Cruising in France

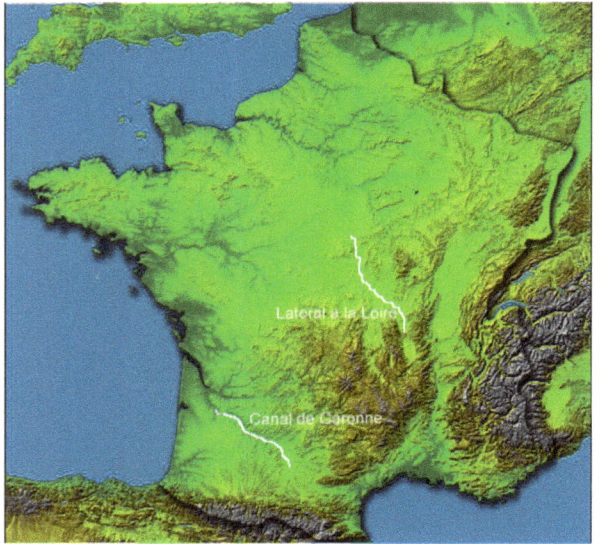

A third type of waterway is a lateral canal, which is an artificial trench that is dug beside the course of a river and fitted with locks. These are built primarily because the course of the river is too sinuous or steep to be easily controlled by weirs and locks within the river bed. The river provides the water to fill the canal and operate its locks. On some lateral canals, in sections where the gentleness of the river allows, the bed of the river is used for navigation and the canal locks into and out of the river. An example of a lateral canal is Canal Latéral de la Loire, which with the branch to Roanne, follows the Loire River for 252 kilometres through 47 locks. Another example is the Canal de Garonne which connects Toulouse to the tidal Garonne at Castets-en-Dorthe, a distance of 193 kilometres with 53 locks.

A fourth type of waterway is the summit canal, which is constructed to cross a pass and connect two watersheds. Because of the necessary climb out of one valley and down into another, many more locks are normally required. The major challenge with a summit canal is to provide a sufficient source of water above the summit to feed the upper pounds so that the canal remains navigable even in the driest seasons. The first summit level canal in France was the Canal de Briare, completed in 1642 using 32 locks in 54 kilometres to connect the basins of the Loire and the Seine. In 1681 le canal royal en Languedoc, which since the French Revolution has been called the Canal du Midi, was completed to connect Toulouse to the Mediterranean using 91 locks over its 240 kilometre length. It rises 189 metres from the Mediterranean to the summit pound then descends 57 metres to the junction with the River Garonne at Toulouse. On both these canals, the final rise to the summit pass is sufficiently gentle that it was practicable to dig the canal directly across the saddle of the pass.

More commonly with a summit canal, the final rise is so steep that it is easier to dig a tunnel through to the other side beneath the top of the pass. On the Canal entre Champagne et Bourgogne there are 114 locks in 224 kilometres with a rise of 239 metres to the summit pound at 341 metres above sea level. The canal then passes through a tunnel 4820 metres long before descending steeply 156 metres through 43 locks in 69 kilometres. The Canal de Bourgogne is another example of a summit level canal. It is the highest canal in France, reaching an elevation of 378 metres above sea level, where it passes through a 3350 metre tunnel. It is also the most lock-intense canal in France, requiring 189 locks in its 240 kilometres.

The oldest known navigational canal is the one that was built approximately 2300 BC to bypass the First Cataract of the Nile at Aswan. The first recorded use of canal locks was in the Canal of the Pharaohs, the first Suez Canal. The canal had been started in the late sixth century BC, linking the Red Sea to the Nile, but it is thought to have remained unfinished until the third century BC when Greek engineers under Ptolemy II devised flash locks to deal with the height differences between the sea and the river. With a flash lock, as the gates are opened, a barge flows through the gap in the weir with the current. Moving upstream against the current requires much more time and effort and spills much more water downstream.

Later, the Romans built many canals, mainly for drainage, irrigation or water supply; however, several were for transportation. In the late first century BC, Fossa Augusta was built to link Ravenna to the Po estuary. Also in the first century BC, in Gaul they linked Narbonne to the Mediterranean and dug canals around Arles for military transport. In 12 BC, also for military purposes, they built Fossa Drusiana to link the Rijn to the Flevomeer, today's IJsselmeer in Friesland. In 47 AD Fossa Corbulonis, a 35-kilometre link was dug to join the Rijn and the Maas without having to go out into the Nordzee. The Foss Dyke in England is thought to have been built around 120 AD by the Romans to connect River Trent to Lincoln. It is likely the oldest canal in Europe that is still in use..

The first recorded use of a pound lock, or chamber lock was in 984 in China. To negotiate a steep decline, two flash locks were built within a short distance of each other. The engineer, Qiao Wei-yo realised he had just devised a system to allow boats to move upstream as easily as down. The pound lock is standard on all modern canals and uses gates at each end of the lock chamber to raise or lower the water taking boats to the level upstream or downstream. Leonardo da Vinci is credited with inventing miter gates in the late fifteenth century. This refinement uses the upstream water pressure to hold the gates tightly closed.

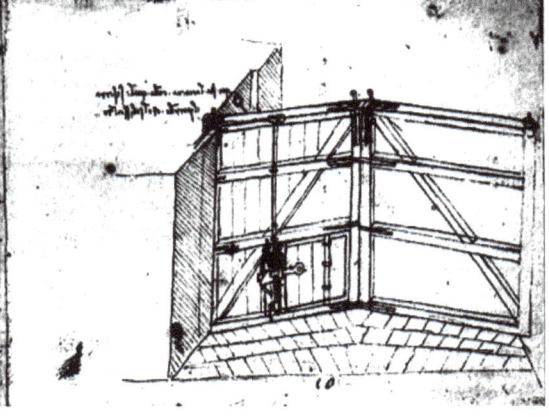

The first pound lock in Europe is believed to be the one built in 1373 in Vreeswijk, Netherlands where the Merwede Canal from Utrecht joins the River Lek. It was used to adjust for the different levels between the river and the canal. In the Netherlands, canal building was primarily done to drain the polders and create dry land, but in so doing, an extensive and efficient inland waterways network evolved and the ease of transportation spurred economic development.

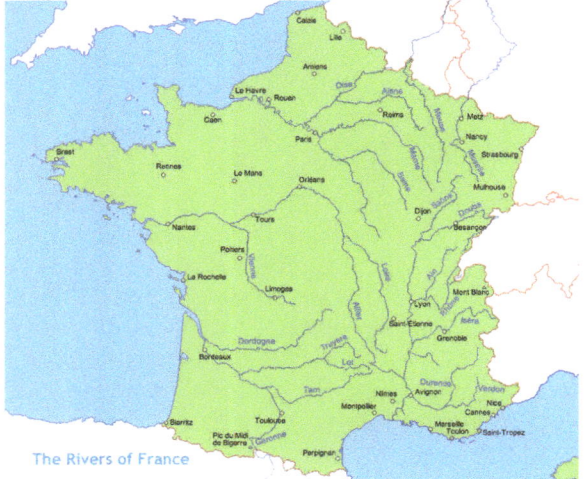

The Rivers of France

In more hilly topography than found in the Netherlands, navigation had been limited to the river valleys, either in the rivers themselves or in works constructed alongside to bypass steep sections. The first canal to break out of a river valley and head over a pass, in what is called a summit level canal, was the Grand Canal of China in the late sixth century AD. It used flash locks.

We have seen that the first summit canal to use pound locks was the Canal de Briare in France, completed in 1642 to connect the basins of the Loire and the Seine. With the completion in 1681 of le canal royal en Languedoc (the Canal du Midi) connecting Toulouse to the Mediterranean, canal construction had reached its maturity. Along its course the canal had passed through the first canal tunnel in Europe and over three major aqueducts spanning river valleys.

During the Middle Ages the transport of goods inland by water cost a tiny fraction of transport overland. A pack horse or mule could carry an eighth of a ton over long distances and on a soft road it could pull a cart of little more than half a ton. The same animal could pull a load of thirty tons on a barge.

The Industrial Revolution spurred a rapid expansion of canal networks across Europe. In Britain, the navigable waterways network grew to keep up with the increasing demand for industrial transportation. A system of large pack horse trains had developed, but few roads at the time could stand up to the heavy wheeled vehicles required to move large amounts of heavy materials. Canal boats were very much quicker, could carry large volumes, and were much safer for fragile items. As the canal network expanded, transportation of raw materials improved, prices fell and this continued to feed the rapid pace of the Industrial Revolution.

From the late eighteenth century, new designs and technology allowed canals to be improved. Where earlier canals had contoured around hills and valleys, later ones went straighter. Locks took canals up and down hills and longer and higher aqueducts spanned broader and deeper valleys. Longer and deeper tunnels pierced the ridges and passes.

In France, canal building continued, with the Canal d'Orleans completed in 1692 to add another link between the Loire and Seine valleys. During the second half of the eighteenth century many canals were begun. In 1789 the Canal du Loing completed the link between the Loire and the Seine through Briare, and in 1794 the Saône was linked to the Loire by completion of the Canal du Centre. The other works in progress were interrupted by the French Revolution and very little happened with them through the Napoleonic era.

With the Restoration after Napoleon's defeat, came a huge public works program. In 1820 François Becquey, Director of Bridges and Highways proposed an immense program of 126 canal and river improvement projects totalling over 25,000 kilometres. Many of these projects were discarded or postponed, but by 1822 Becquey had pushed bills through the French legislature authorizing the finance, construction and operation of ten new waterways. Another 2000 kilometres were built. By the time of the abdication of King Louis Philippe in 1848, France had more than 10,000 kilometres of navigable inland waterways. During the last third of the nineteenth century, another 3000 kilometres of canals were upgraded or completed and 4000 kilometres of rivers had improvements to navigation.

Among the major works: the Rhine and Saône were linked by a canal over the southern Vosges in 1834, the Seine and Saône were linked in 1842 by the Canal de Bourgogne, the Marne and Rhine were linked in 1853 over the northern Vosges, and in 1856 the Canal Lateral à la Garonne eased navigation from Toulouse to Bordeaux. Also constructed during the first half of the nineteenth century were canals leading northward into Germany, Belgium and the North Sea. A canal linking the Marne and the Saône was begun in 1870 and completed in 1907. At this point, the French network reached its greatest extent with 12,778 kilometres of navigable inland waterways.

From the mid-nineteenth century, the expanding railway network began replacing canals.. As rail transportation became more advanced, land transportation became cheaper and faster. To deal with the decline in canal usage, the engineer, Charles-Louis Freycinet as Minister of Public Works in 1879 began a standardization of the waterway network that had been built over the previous three centuries. He saw that the large variety of lock dimensions was impeding efficient commerce, so he began a rebuilding project that by 1913 had refitted over 1500 kilometres of canals to standard dimensions. These have been called Gabarit Freycinet, the Freycinet Gauge and call for locks sized to handle barges with maximum dimensions of 38.50 meters length, 5.05 metres beam and 1.8 metres draft. Low bridges were rebuilt to allow for a minimum clearance of 3.5 metres.

After World War I the commercial transportation in much of Western Europe increasingly went to rail and road and the economic viability of many of the canals steadily declined. Their decreasing use meant reduced revenues for maintenance and they fell into disrepair. Many became non-navigable and were closed. Some were filled-in. In France between 1926 and 1957 nearly 5000 kilometres of navigable waterways were closed or abandoned.

There remain today in France ninety-four navigable rivers and canals with a total length of 8800 kilometres and 2165 locks. Of these, 8300 kilometres are interconnected across the northern part of the country, down its eastern side and across its southwest. More than three-quarters of these are Class I and lower with minimal commercial traffic and are ideally suited to pleasure cruising.

Chapters Two

The Regions of France

France has a very complex and divided administrative bureaucracy. The main portion of the country, which is located in Western Europe is often referred to as Metropolitan France. Metropolitan France is divided into ninety-six administrative units, called Départements. In addition there are Départements d'Outre Mers, Overseas Départements, which include French Guyana, Martinique and Guadeloupe in the Caribbean and Réunion and Mayotte in the Indian Ocean. There are also Overseas Territories and Overseas Collectivities, such as French Polynesia and Saint Pierre and Miquelon. Each of the Départements is run from a Préfecture and each Département is divided into Arrondissements, which are further divided into Cantons.

In 1982 in an attempt to simplify the administrative tangle, the ninety-six Départements of Metropolitan France were formally grouped into twenty-two Régions. These consist of from two to eight Départements each. Many of the Régions took the names of historic duchies of France, such as Burgundy, Aquitaine, Normandy, Alsace and Brittany and many of their current boundaries approximated those of medieval times. The Régions lack legislative authority and therefore cannot write their own statutory law; their primary responsibility is to build and run high schools and promote la Région.

Canal Cruising in France

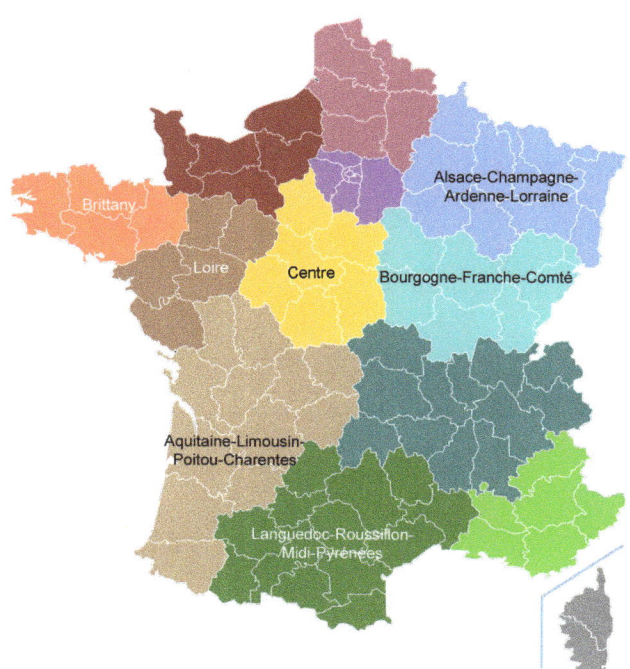

In 2014, the French National Assembly and the Senate passed a law that will reduce the number of regions in Metropolitan France from twenty-two to thirteen. The new Régions will take effect on 1 January 2016. Six of the current Régions are unaffected by the consolidation, while the remaining sixteen are regrouped into seven larger administrative units. The names of the newly created Régions are for the most part merely hyphenated forms of the old names, such of the as Burgogne-Franche-Comté and Alsace-Lorraine-Champagne-Ardennes. Observers think that after the adoption of the new Régions, the French will continue to refer to their separate parts. Burgundy will still be Burgundy, Alsace will still be Alsace and Champagne will still be Champagne. For this reason, I will switch back and forth between the pre-2016 and the post 2016 names.

The areas of France with the most interesting canal and river cruising are in the Alsace-Lorraine, the Aquetaine, Brittany, the Burgundy-Franche-Comté, the Loire and the Midi. It is not surprising, therefore, that the largest number of canal boat rental bases are located in those areas. There are about four dozen canal boat rental companies in France, including four major ones. The largest of these is Le Boat, followed closely by Canalous then Nicols and Locaboat. Each of these companies has rental bases in the most popular areas.

A major consideration when renting a boat is the ability to pick it up at one base and at the end of the cruise, drop it off in another location. Most of the large operators have multiple bases in each of the areas, making it an easy option to explore more without needing to retrace routes.

In Alsace-Lorraine-Champagne-Ardennes, Canalous has four bases, Le Boat three and Nicols and Locaboat two each. Most of these are in the Alsace, which in many ways is a world-apart from the remainder of France. With its Germanic influence, the language, architecture, culture and cuisine developed along quite different paths. The historical language, Alsatian is spoken in Lorraine and across the Rhine in Germany, but today most Alsatians speak French, the official language of France. In 2010, 43 percent of the adult population spoke Alsatian but only three percent of those under seventeen years old did.

	Le Boat	Canalous	Nicols	Locaboat
ALSACE-LORRAINE				
Boofzheim	■			
Harskirchen			■	
Hochfelden		■		
Hesse	■			
Languimberg		■		
Lutzelbourg	■			■
Pont-à-Bar		■		
Niderviller		■		
Saverne			■	

10

The Regions of France

In the Aquitaine-Charente the major operators have a total of twelve rental bases. These are broadly dispersed, giving good access to the Canal de Garonne, the Canal de Montech and the Rivers Charente, Baïse and Lot. The Charente flows through the heart of the Cognac vineyards and past the producers of one of the world's great brandies. The Baïse flows through the centre of Armagnac, the other famous French brandy. Cruises along the Lot River pass prehistoric sites and spectacular medieval towns and villages. Along the Canal de Garonne are many more medieval sites steeped in history, among them is a near-forgotten Rembrandt painting hanging in an old village church.

Brittany offers a strong cultural change from the remainder of France. Originally populated from Great Britain during the Anglo-Saxon conquests fifteen hundred years ago, the people have evolved a language, Breton, which is related to Welsh and Cornish and in the eastern portion there is another language, Gallo. Brittany did not become a part of France until 1532 and today most speak the official French language. The major rental companies operate a total of eight bases in the region and offer itineraries that wind through quiet rural settings and past towering castles and cobblestoned villages. Being close to the Atlantic coast, the fish is superb and abundant, both in the markets and in the restaurants.

With twenty-four rental bases among the big four companies, the Burgundy-Franche-Comté is one of the major destinations for canal cruisers. The Saône River flows from north to south through the centre of the region and offers relaxed navigation with few locks and many historic towns and cities. The Canal du Centre, Canal de Bourgogne and Canal de Nivernais run near or past the great wine regions such as Côte d'Or, Côte Chalonais and Chablis and through a region that was the centre of European art and culture before the Italian Renaissance. The wines are superb, the cuisine is delicious and the scenery is magnificent.

	Le Boat	Canalous	Nicols	Locaboat
AQUITAINE				
Agen				✓
Bouzies			✓	
Buzet-sur-Baïse				✓
Cahors		✓		
Castelsarassin	✓	✓		
Cognac		✓		
Douelle			✓	
Fourques-Sur-Garonne	✓			
Jarnac			✓	
Luzech			✓	
Mas d'Agenais	✓			
Sireiul			✓	
BRITTANY				
Dinan			✓	
Glenac			✓	
Messac		✓		
Nort-sur-Erdre			✓	
Redon	✓			
Saint Martin sur Oust				✓
Suce-sur-Erdre			✓	
BURGUNDY				
Branges	✓			
Briare				✓
Châtel-Censoir	✓			
Brienon			✓	
Châtillon-en-Bazois		✓		
Chatillon-sur-Loire		✓		
Coulanges sur Yonne		✓		
Decize		✓		
Digoin		✓		
Dole			✓	
Fontenoy-le-Chateau	✓			
Gray	✓			
Joigny				✓
Louhans		✓		
Mâcon			✓	
Migennes	✓			
Montbard				✓
Plagny			✓	
Pontailler-sur-Saône		✓		
Port-sur-Saône			✓	
Rogny		✓		
Saint-Florentin				*
Saint-Jean-de-Losne	✓			
Saint-Léger-sur-Dheune				✓
Tannay	✓			
Venarey			✓	
Vermenton				*

	Le Boat	Canalous	Nicols	Locaboat
LOIRE				
Chenillé-Changé		✓		
Châteauneuf-sur-Sarthe		✓		
Daon		✓		
Grez-Neuville			✓	
Le Mans		✓		
Sablé-sur-Sarthe			✓	
MIDI				
Agde				
Argens				✓
Beaucaire	✓			
Bellegarde			✓	
Capestang				✓
Carcassonne				
Carnon				
Castelnaudary	✓			
Colombiers	✓			
Homps	✓			
Lattes				✓
Le Somail			✓	
Narbonne	✓			
Négra				✓
Port Cassafiéres	✓			
Port Lauragais			✓	
Saint-Gilles	✓			
Trèbes	✓			

The Loire River flows through the western part of the Burgundy, through the Centre region and out to the Atlantic through the Anjou. For simplicity here, we will divide the area in two: western portion near the Burgundy with superb goat cheese and Sauvignn Blanc will be considered with the Burgundy. The Anjou portion will be treated as the Loire. Two of the four major boat rental companies have bases in six locations along the Sarthe and Mayenne Rivers and offer cruising options as varied as the area. There are winding rivers, huge, sprawling châteaux, medieval villages and large cities.

The Midi is steeped in history and prehistory. Some of the oldest cities in France are here, including Béziers, which dates to 575 BC and Agde from 525 BC. The Romans occupied, rebuilt and defended these cities and others in the following centuries and their traces are seen near everywhere through the region. The Canal du Midi opened in 1681 and is listed as a UNESCO World Heritage site. Most of its locks and humpbacked bridges along its course are the original seventeenth century structures. The canal runs through famous wine regions, such as Minervois, Corbières and Limoux, the food is deliciously rustic and the climate is sunny. July and August are hot and very crowded; the preferred times are spring and autumn. The four major companies have twenty-one rental bases here, distributed from one end to the other.

The four major companies have nearly two-thirds of the boat rental bases in France and the remaining third is divided among some forty other companies that provide rental boats on the French inland waterways. Most of these have one base, a few have two or three, but none approach the big four in diversity or numbers. There is also a large number of companies that act as booking agents for one, two or many of the rental companies.

While the geography of France is very diverse and varies greatly from region to region, your choice of where to explore will likely depend less on the geography than it will on what history, culture, wine or cuisine interests you. These are even more complex and varied across the regions than is the geography. Important in this is the ease of access from your rental boat to the finer examples of what interests you and what you want to enjoy: the museums, the galleries, the monumental buildings, the medieval villages, the historic town centres, the wine producers, the typical restaurants and the fine dining meccas. Public transportation in rural France and even in its towns and villages is less available and less dependable than it is elsewhere in the world. Rental cars, taxis, bicycles and foot will be your main side-trip options.

Let's go look at each of the regions in a little more detail. Alsace is located on the eastern border of France, across the barrier of the Vosges Mountains from the remainder of the country. It lies along the west bank of the upper Rhine River across from Germany and Switzerland. With its strategic location on the Rhine and the protection from west offered by the Vosges mountains, Alsace has long been a target of conquest and its evolution through the centuries has been heavily influenced by wars, and strategic politics. Strasbourg is the political, economic and cultural capital of Alsace and the region's largest city. Strasbourg is the seat of many international organizations and bodies, including the Council of Europe, the European Court of Human Rights and European Parliament. It is often referred to as the European Capital.

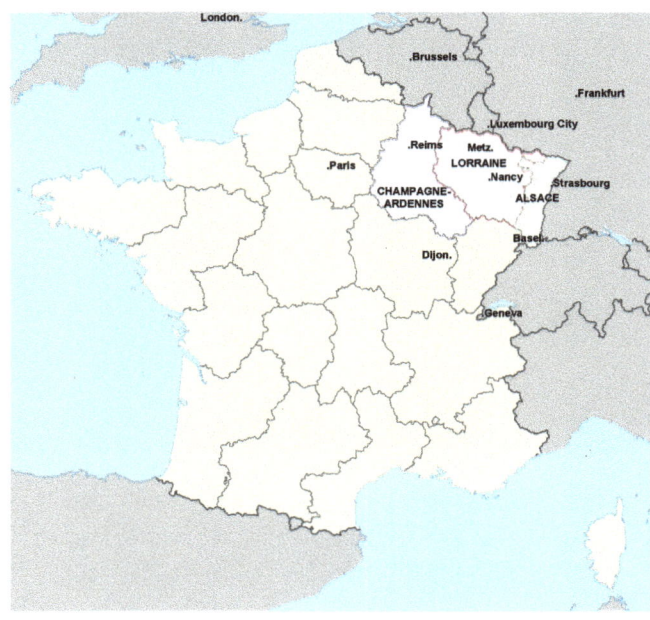

Across the flat plains bordering the Rhine and up into the eastern foothills of the Vosges Mountains begin the vineyards that make Alsace famous internationally as one of the world's great wine producers. A few wonderfully preserved medieval towns and villages survived the ravages of the Second World War. Some of these seem stuffed into the narrow Vosges valleys on patches of flat lands at the edges of the vineyard slopes, just beyond the last pieces of soil that could sustain fine vineyards. The Alsace wines are made from seven grape varieties, the Riesling, Gewürztraminer, Pinot Gris, Pinot Blanc, Muscat and Sylvaner being white and the Pinot Noir a red. The whites are characterized as being aromatic, floral and spicy and most are made in a crisply dry style, often with a delicious minerality and fruity lusciousness. Wonderfully complex desert wines are made from late harvest grapes and superb ones from hand selected super-ripe grapes. These last are rare and expensive. One of the great sparkling wines of France is Crémant d'Alsace, which is made in the same method as the great wines of Champagne. It is one of the best quality/price values of France.

In 1870 the newly founded German Empire annexed the entire Alsace and the northern section of Lorraine, which were both largely German-speaking. The French language was forbidden until after the First World War, when in 1919 France regained the territories. The French then banned the use of the German language and expelled Germans who had moved into the area after 1871. In 1940 Germany re-annexed Alsace-Lorraine and the French regained it in November 1944.

Twenty-five years ago while I was conducting a wine and food tour through the Alsace, one of the greatest winemakers of the era, Jean Hugel told us: "My mother was born in France, then lived in Germany and then in France again and then in Germany and she died living in France. She never moved from this house in Riquewihr, where she was born".

Bordering Alsace to the west, with the watershed of the Vosges as the boundary, is Lorraine. To its north, Lorraine borders on Germany, Luxembourg and Belgium and on its east it abuts the Champagne-Ardennes of France. The former Duchy of Lorraine remained outside France until the eighteenth century. It was under Germanic control for centuries and was coveted and fought for by neighbouring France and Burgundy. The last Duke of Burgundy was killed in the Battle of Nancy in 1477 during an attempt to conquer Lorraine. In 1766 Lorraine was annexed by France and reorganized as a province. There are three languages spoken here: Lorraine Franconian is a Germanic dialect spoken by a minority in the northern Lorraine and the Alsatian language is spoken by some in the east portion, near the border with Alsace. Neither of these languages has any form of official recognition, the official language being French.

Northern Lorraine was once focused on mining and metallurgy with vast coal fields and iron mines and the industrial complexes necessary for their extraction and conversion. The dirty industries have been in decline for decades and now form only a small portion of the economy, over two-thirds of which comes from the service sector. Geologically, Lorraine lies in the Paris Basin with rivers draining northward and westward and there are delightful areas of lakes and streams.

The Regions of France

Most of the boat rental bases in the region are in the slopes of the Vosges Mountains straddling the border between Alsace and Lorraine. The four major companies have nine of their eleven bases inside a fifty kilometre circle here This compact area is crammed full of wondrous places to see and explore. Prime among these is the inclined boat lift at Arzviller, which is unique in Europe, lifting a tank full of boats up a slope and replacing the former series of seventeen locks and saving a full day of travel for boats and barges.

Beyond the amazing infrastructure of the canals with their locks, tunnels and aqueducts, there is much to see. There are castles looking down from seemingly impossible perches on steep hilltops and ridges, there are lush forests with fairytale villages, there are battlefield monuments and war cemeteries. And everywhere there are gastronomic delights; whether you choose choucroute garnie or foie gras, quiche lorraine or flammekueche, Munster cheese, kougelhopf or baba au rhum, there are great Alsace wines to complement them all. And don't forget the beer; Alsace is the main beer producing region in France. There are vast hops vineyards here, which are used not only by the large international breweries, but also many small craft breweries. The region is among the more prosperous in France and the people are very cheerful and welcoming.

Out of the Vosges Mountains and into the more gentle rolling hills Lorraine there are winding rivers that wander through peaceful towns and villages filled with half-timbered houses. The Meurthe River flows northwestward through Nancy, the largest city in Lorraine then empties into the Moselle River, which continues northward into Germany through Metz, the capital of Lorraine. These two offer big city flair and old world charm, while much of the remainder of the old province remains rural and undeveloped. The Meuse River flows northward through the western portion of the old province then bends to head into Belgium. Navigation follows the courses of these rivers and there are canals that link them together into a network of inland waterways.

To the west of Lorraine is the Champagne-Ardennes, where in Pont à Bar there are two boat rental bases. The distance from the base to the Champagne wine region requires a two week rental to make the trip feasible and even then, much of the trip to and from the wine region is spent cruising through sparsely populated areas, where other than the battlefields, monuments and cemeteries from the two World Wars, there are few attractions compared to much of the remainder of France.

The Regions of France

Bordering on the south of the Alsace-Lorraine-Champagne-Ardennes region is the Burgundy-Franche-Comté. With its total of twenty-seven rental bases among the big four companies, this region offers the widest selection of navigation itineraries in France. It is a very complex region, with wheat fields, and dense forests, great vineyards, fields of chickens and pastures of cattle. Agriculture is the central theme here as it has been for more than two thousand years.

There are broad river valleys: the Doubs flows through Franche-Comté from the Vosges at the edge of the Alsace and empties into the Saône in the Burgundy; the Saône rises in the Vosges and flows southwestward from the Lorraine on its way to the Rhône and the Mediterranean, and the Loire flows northward along the western portion of the Burgundy on its way from the Massif Central to the Atlantic. Navigation along these rivers dates back many centuries and engineering through the nineteenth and twentieth centuries made the navigation easier.

A network of canals interconnects these river valleys to others, making it possible to head in six different directions from a hub in Saint-Jean-de-Losne. This is one of the attractions to cruising in this region; there are so many choices of places to go. From the hub you can head down the broad Saône with very few locks leading past wonderful towns and villages. You can head southwestward across the Canal du Centre close past the vineyards of Chassagne Montrachet, Santenay and Rully on the way across to the Loire Valley. You can head northwestward up Canal de Bourgogne through historic Dijon into the beautiful Val d'Ouche and past exquisite villages and medieval hilltop towns, and if you chose continue over the summit, you can from there head down toward the valleys of the Yonne and the Seine. Northeastward from the hub will lead you into the valley of the Doubs through Dole and fortified city of Besançon on the way up the Vosges and into the Alsace. North and then northeastward up the Saône offers gentle cruising with few locks leading through pastoral settings dotted with historic places, such as Auxonne and Gray and you can continue up into the Lorraine. Along the way you can chose to turn north and continue along the canal that leads to the Marne Valley and the Champagne.

To make it easy for renters to explore the region, the four largest boat rental companies have twenty-seven bases rather evenly spread through the most popular areas. Le Boat has nine bases, Locaboat has seven, Nicols has six and Canalous has five. Thus each of the major companies make it easy to plan cruising itineraries from base to base without the need to retrace routes.

Among the must-sees in the Burgundy is Musée des Beaux-Arts in Dijon. Forgotten in the modern hype about the Italian Renaissance is the fact that fine art and cultured life were thriving in the Burgundy long before the cobwebs began being stirred in Florence and Venice. During the fourteenth and fifteenth centuries, Dijon was the centre of European art and culture. The Burgundy in the mid-fifteenth century was the most powerful and prosperous place in Europe, and arguably, the world. Musée des Beaux-

Canal Cruising in France

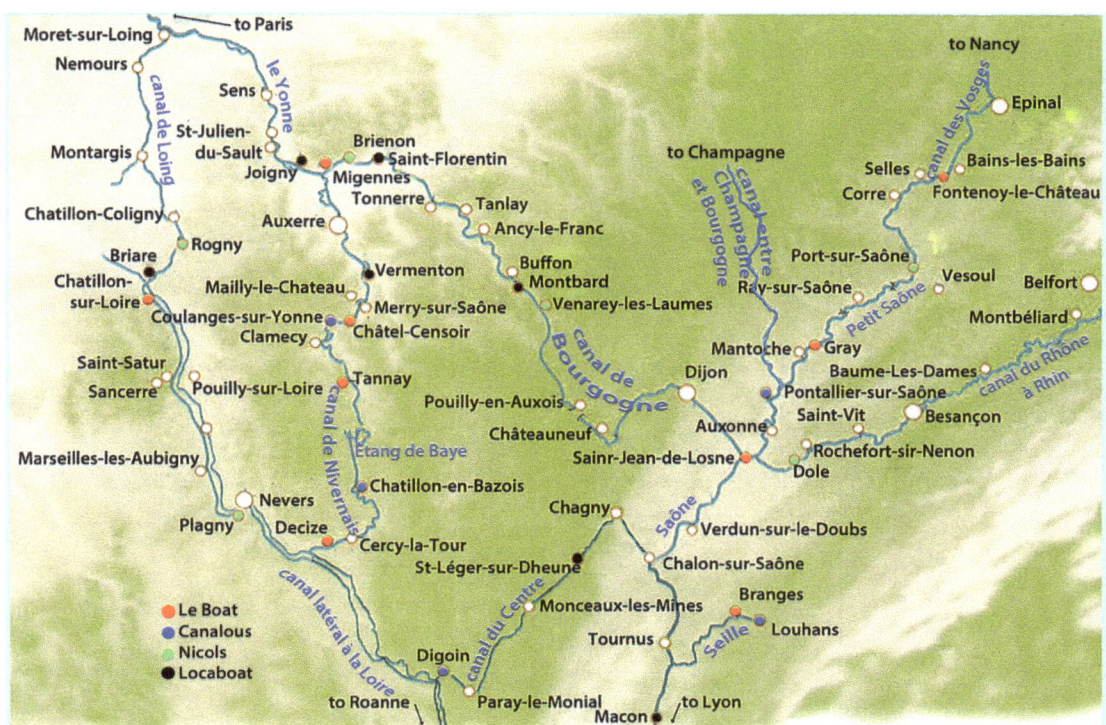

Arts is one of the most important museums in France and it is located in the former palace of Dukes of Burgundy. Admission is free. In it are ancient Egyptian, Greek, Etruscan, Gallic, Roman and Byzantine displays, but of greater interest are the displays of Burgundian art, including paintings by the Dutch and Flemish masters, from the days when the Burgundy owned, ruled and influenced the areas we now know as Belgium and the Netherlands. We are reminded that the Burgundian Netherlands introduced oil paints to Italy around 1460.

Work on this tomb of Duke Philip the Bold was begun in 1381 and completed in 1410;. it is recognized as one of the finest examples of early Burgundian sculpture. Even finer and more imposing is the tomb of Philip's son and heir, Duke John the Fearless. The museum is an easy tram ride or a pleasant walk from the mooring basin through the heart of the medieval city. Nearby are vestiges of the third century Roman walls that were built to fortify the city. The old covered market is just around the corner and it was designed by Gustave Eiffel of Tower fame. It is alive with commerce on market days: Tuesday, Friday and Saturday.

Across the summit of Canal de Bourgogne and through the 3.3 kilometre tunnel and down the other side are many delightful towns oozing with the history of medieval Burgundy. In Tonnerre is the largest medieval hospital in Europe, built and donated to the people in 1295 by Marguerite de Bourgogne, who was Countess of Tonnerre and Queen of Sicily, Naples and Jerusalem. Along the way are castles to explore, quaint villages to wander and gentle rolling countryside to enjoy.

At the end of Canal de Bourgogne is the Yonne River and a short distance up its gentle course is the old city of Auxerre, which traces its roots to Roman settlements and became a provincial capital in the Roman Empire. An early Christian centre, it received its first bishop in the third century and a cathedral in the fifth. The medieval city gate, Tour de l'Horloge was built on portions of third and fourth century Roman city walls. The vineyards of the Chablis, Irancy and Saint Bris regions are close by for tours and tastings.

The Canal du Nivernais runs from Auxerre up and across a pass and then down to the Loire River at Decize. Often called the most beautiful canal in France, the Nivernais was begun in the 1780s, and after interruptions by the French Revolution and the Napoleonic Wars, it was opened in 1843. It is among the few canals in France not upgraded to standard dimensions in the late nineteenth and early twentieth century. Its low bridges and shallow depth make commercial traffic uneconomic and it is now used almost exclusively by pleasure boaters.

The canal follows the course of the Yonne up to three tunnels at the summit and then follows along the smaller Aron River down the other side. Along the way the canal flows mainly through pastoral settings, with a sprinkling of delightful small towns and villages. There are few large communities along the route and the atmosphere is peaceful and relaxing as you cruise past grazing Charolais cattle in the rolling pastures along the banks of the canal.

At Decize the Canal du Nivernais ends in the Loire River. A short distance along, two locks take boats up and down between the river and the Canal Latéral à la Loire. The Loire is the longest river in France, rising in the Massif Central only 150 kilometres from the Mediterranean and flowing in a great arc 1012 kilometres across France to the Atlantic and on

the way draining over one fifth of land area of the country. Navigation along 950 kilometres of its course goes back many centuries, but in the 1830s a lateral canal was opened to make this much easier along the upper third of the river from Briare to Roanne.

Downstream from Decize the canal gently descends through only twenty-two locks in its 132 kilometre passage to Briare. Along the way it passes Nevers, which dates to a Roman stronghold established by Julius Caesar in 52 BC. The canal passes under the great vineyards of Sancerre and through the famous goat cheese region of Chavignol. At Briare is the 662-metre-long aqueduct over the Loire River. The piers and abutments were designed and built by Gustave Eiffel and the structure was opened to navigation in 1896. For more than a century it was the world's longest canal aqueduct and it had been built to obviate the need to descend through locks and cross the heavy current of the river before locking back up the

other side. The canal bridge links the Canal Latéral à la Loire with the Canal de Briare., which opened in 1642 as the first summit level canal in Europe. The Briare canal ascends through fourteen locks to the summit at Rogny before descending toward the Seine River basin, which leads to Paris.

Heading upstream from Decize the Canal Latéral à la Loire also follows a gentle course through only fifteen locks in sixty-eight kilometres to its junction with the Canal du Centre at Digoin. Just short of Digoin a branch continues south for fifty-six kilometres through ten locks to the city of Roanne at the head of Loire navigation.

From Digoin the Canal du Centre leads northeastward to the Saône River at Chalon-sur-Saône. This is another beautiful and peaceful canal, particularly on the Loire side of the pass. The small cities of Paray-le Monial and Monceau-les-Mines are well worth a visit and there is a delightfully quiet mooring basin at Genelard. The locks are designated as Océan or Mediterranée, since the summit is the watershed between the Atlantic and the Mediterranean.

Heading down the Mediterranée side through small, quiet towns and villages and past the Pinot Noir and Chardonnay vineyards of the Côte d'Or the canal arrives in Chagny. The large mooring basin is a bit grubby, but it is a great jumping-off spot to tour the vineyards and winemakers of the Côte de Beaune and the Côte Chalonnaise. A few blocks from the moorings is one of the greatest restaurants in France. Pierre Lameloise received his second Michelin star in 1931 and in 1979 his grandson, Jacques received a third star. Jacques Lameloise cooked for me many times throughout the 1980s and 90s on my travels in the Burgundy searching for wines to import. A new chef is in the kitchen, but the three stars remain, so long advance reservations are a must.

Entering the Saône River at the end of the canal and turning right quickly leads to the wonderful city of Chalon-sur-Saône. There are ancient winding streets to explore and street markets set-up on Wednesday, Friday and Sunday. Thirty kilometres downstream is another medieval riverside city, Tournus, which is another very pleasant place to stop, as is Macon a further thirty kilometres downstream.

Six kilometres south of Tournus is the mouth of the Seille River. The winding river is navigable thirty-nine kilometres upstream through four locks to the city of Louhans. This takes you eastward into the heart of the Bresse region of the Burgundy, famous for its chickens. Poulet de Bresse is renowned for its gamey depth of flavour and fine tender flesh. Prolonged rain is common in the area and the central district boasts 157 arcades to keep shoppers dry. The river is subject to flooding in any season, so sometimes it is necessary to pause a day or so to wait for the current to ease. It is a great place to wait.

Back out on the Saône, the river flows southward to Lyon and the junction with the Rhône River, which leads down to the Mediterranean and the Midi. The Saône northward from Saint-Jean-de-Losne passes through Auxonne, a very strategic fortified city in medieval times, being Burgundian but sited on the 'enemy' side of the river. More recently, Napoleon Bonaparte twice trained in the military garrison here as a young lieutenant before going on to greater things. The river is broad here and the current is gentle during prime cruising season making navigation easy and pleasant.

Thirty kilometres upstream from Auxonne past the pleasant towns of Lamarche and Pontallier is the junction with le canal entre Champagne et Bourgogne, the canal between Champagne and Burgundy. It leads steeply up forty-three locks in sixty-nine kilometres to a tunnel nearly five kilometres long before heading down the other side through seventy-one locks toward the Marne, giving access to the Champagne and Paris. Continuing up the Saône another twenty-eight kilometres leads to the city of Gray in the Franche-Comté. The market sets-up here on Friday mornings.

From Gray onward up the Saône, the communities are smaller and more scattered and the river winds through forests and fields another hundred-and-twenty kilometres to its end of navigation and the junction with Canal des Vosges, which leads into the Lorraine. Because its locks are the smaller Freycinet gauge of 38.5 x 5.05 x 1.8 metres, the section of the Saône northward from Saint-Jean-de-Losne is called le Petit Saône, to differentiate it from the section south of Saint-Jean-de-Losne with locks 185 x 12 x 3.35 metres in size all the way downstream to Lyon.

Just four kilometres up the Saône from Saint-Jean-de-Losne is the junction with le Canal de Rhône au Rhin, the canal from the Rhône to the Rhine. This leads through the Franche-Comte and up across the southern end of the Vosges Mountains into the Alsace. In doing so, the canal climbs through sixty-one locks in a hundred-and sixty-five kilometres. For one-hundred-and-twenty kilometres of this, the route follows the Doubs River, frequently transiting in and out between the river itself and a lateral canal. The great engineering that accomplished this was begun in 1784 and completed in 1834.

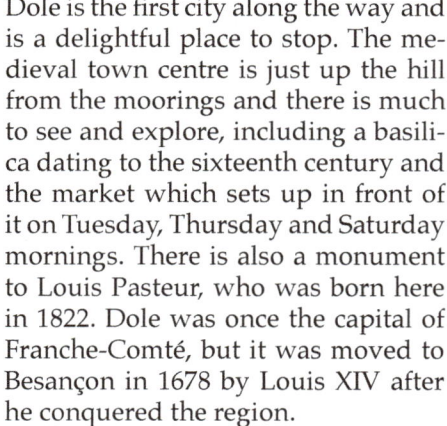

Dole is the first city along the way and is a delightful place to stop. The medieval town centre is just up the hill from the moorings and there is much to see and explore, including a basilica dating to the sixteenth century and the market which sets up in front of it on Tuesday, Thursday and Saturday mornings. There is also a monument to Louis Pasteur, who was born here in 1822. Dole was once the capital of Franche-Comté, but it was moved to Besançon in 1678 by Louis XIV after he conquered the region.

Besançon is fifty-four kilometres upstream from Dole and is sited in an enviable strategic location in a sharp buckle of the Doubs. The site was settled more than 3500 years ago by tribes of Celts and the settlement was first recorded by Julius Caesar in 58 BC. In 843 the Treaty of Verdun placed the city and the region around it under the control of the Duke of Burgundy. In 1043 it became a free city-state in the Holy Roman Empire and it was granted total independence in 1290. It came again under the influence of the Dukes of Burgundy in the fifteenth century and with the marriage of Duchess Mary of Burgundy to Maximilian I, its influence passed to the Holy Roman Emperor. When Emperor Charles V abdicated in 1555, he gave Besançon to his son, Philip II, King of Spain. It remained a free imperial city under the protection of the King of Spain until in 1598 when Philip II gave the province to his daughter on her marriage to an Austrian archduke. It then remained formally a portion of the Austrian Empire until the Peace of Westphalia in 1648 when Spain regained control of Franche-Comté and the city lost its status as a free city.

Then in 1667, Louis XIV of France claimed the province as a consequence of his marriage to Marie-Thérèse of Spain. Louis took possession of the city in 1668, but the Treaty of Aix-la-Chapelle returned it to Spain within a few months. While it was in French control the great military engineer,

Vauban drew-up plans for its fortification. As soon as the Spaniards regained control, they following Vauban's plans and quickly built la Citadelle, the centre point of the city's defences. It was placed atop Mont Saint-Étienne, a site nearly encircled by the oxbow in the river, the site of the original town more than three millennia previously. In 1674, French troops recaptured the city, and four years later the Treaty of Nijmegen awarded the city to France. Who said European history is simple?

Southward down the Saône and Rhône takes boaters to the Midi, one of the most popular cruising areas of France. Because of the heavy commercial traffic and the fast river currents that are possible on the Rhône, the rental companies do not take the risk of offering boats along the Rhône, nor do they allow their boats to navigate on it. Approximately eighteen hundred private pleasure boats with owners from nearly two dozen different countries make the trip up or down the river between Saône and the Midi each year.

The word 'midi' in French means 'noon' and since at least the middle ages, it has colloquially referred to the South, the position of the noonday sun; the South of France has been known as le Midi for centuries. Among inland boaters, however, le Midi usually means le canal du Midi.

The canal connects the Étang de Thau on the Mediterranean to the inland city of Toulouse. Construction began in 1666 and it was completed in 1681. Initially it was named canal royal en Languedoc, but with anti-royal sentiment during the French Revolution in 1789 it was renamed canal du Midi. In 1996 it was named as a UNESCO World Heritage Site and described as: "one of the most remarkable feats of civil engineering in modern times".

Also considered as a part of the boating scene in the Midi is the canal du Rhône à Sète, which runs through the low dunes that separate the Mediterranean from the brackish lagoons that rim the low lands along the coast. This canal runs through the Camargue with only one lock in the ninety-eight kilometres between Beaucaire on the Rhone and the Mediterranean seaside port of Sète, which backs on Étang de Thau.

Canal Cruising in France

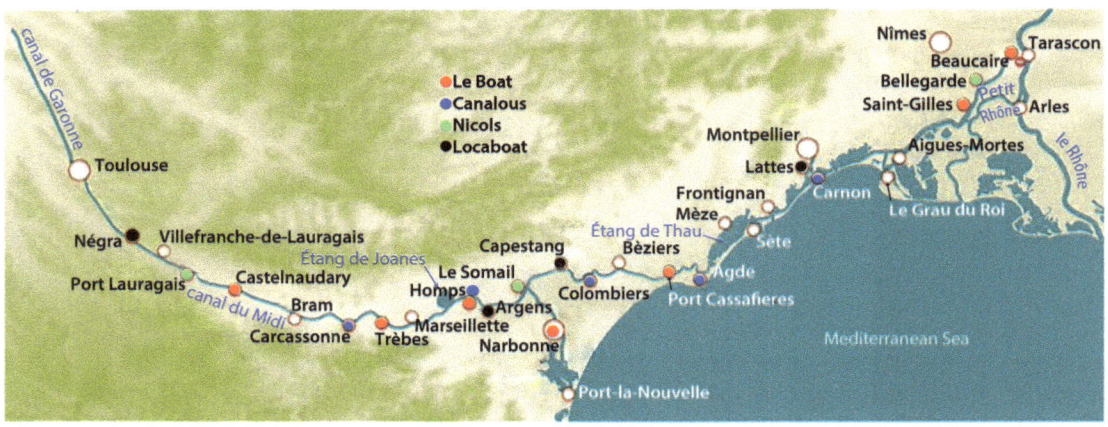

The four major rental companies have eighteen bases across the Midi. Five bases are on le canal du Rhône à Sète across the Camargue and along the étangs between Beaucaire and Sète. Ten are along the climb of the Canal du Midi from sea level at the edge of the Mediterranean to its summit. Two are on the western slope of the Canal du Midi on its way down to Toulouse and one is down a branch canal in Narbonne. Le Boat operates seven of these bases, Canalous has five, Locaboat four and Nicols three. Each company has their bases distributed to make it easy to organize base-to-base itineraries without the need to retrace routes.

Settlement at Beaucaire, at the northern end of Midi navigation, dates to the seventh century BC. In the second century BC the city became an important depot on the Roman road that linked Italy with Spain. The city oozes history, and around it are spectacular Roman sites to see, such as Pont de Gard, Nimes and Arles. Heading down le canal du Rhône à Sète takes boats through the Camargue, famous for its wild horses. Horse breeding is a very important activity here and it is common so see herds along the canal.

Out of the Camargue and into the étangs, the scenery changes dramatically. The salt water ponds and marshes on the inland side are home to flamingos, while the low grassy dunes on the other side separate the canal from the Mediterranean. There are coastal resort communities all along and it is also possible to stop in the wilds to take a dip in the Sea.

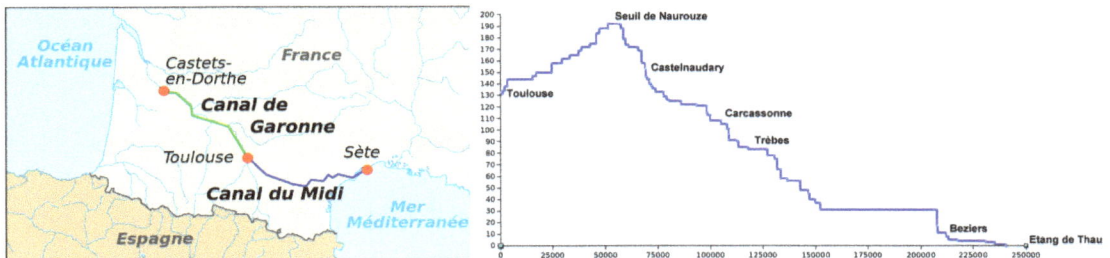

Across Étang de Thau is the beginning of le canal du Midi. The inspiration and driving force behind its construction was Pierre-Paul Riquet and at the time it was widely praised as one of the great achievements of the seventeenth century. The canal rises 189.4 metres through 74 locks over a distance of 183.5 kilometres to a 5 kilometre summit pound. From there it descends 57.18 metres through 17 locks in 51.6 kilometres to Toulouse, where it connects to the Canal de Garonne and then the Garonne River, which leads past Bordeaux to the Atlantic.

Most of the locks on the Canal du Midi have curved sided chambers, though a few have been rebuilt with parallel sides. The original dimensions of the chambers are 29.2 metres long with a maximum width of 11 metres at the centres. The entrances past the doors are 5.8 metres wide, the design principal being to allow two 20-metre barges of 5 metres width to easily fit into the lock simultaneously. The average height change of the locks is 2.1 metres. Although manoeuvring a boat into and out of these looks initially looks tricky, after learning the tricks with the first two or three, it is easy.

Amazingly, much of the original engineering work from the seventeenth century is still in use. Besides the wonderful masonry of the locks, all along the canal are stone spillways to shed excess water and aqueducts to carry the canal over streams and rivers, some of these with structures to keep the hooves and feet of the barge haulers dry. Most of the original humpback bridges still carry traffic across the canal after nearly three and a half centuries.

Agde is the first large community along the canal. It is one of the oldest towns in France, having been settled in 525 BC by Greeks from Massilia, modern-day Marseilles, which itself had been established by the Greeks in 600 BC. Up canal twenty-four kilometres is Béziers, the second oldest town in France, founded in 575 BC. Its site has been occupied since Neolithic times, before the influx of Celts. The Romans built their road linking Italy to Spain through here and they re-established the city as a colony for veterans in 35 BC. It is a marvellous city to explore.

A short distance beyond the 375-metre aqueduct, which carries the canal across the Orb River, is one of the most touristed sites of the canal. L'échelle de Fonserannes is a staircase of seven interconnected locks that take boats up and down the steep hillside on the west side of the Orb. There were originally nine locks in the flight, but with the construction of the aqueduct in 1856, the final two down into the river were no longer needed. Boats now enter through the side of the seventh chamber.

At the top of the staircase begins a fifty-four kilometre pound to the next lock. Here the canal winds a sinuous path around hillsides and stream valleys at thirty-three metres above sea level. Seven kilometres along is le tunnel de Malpas, which was the first canal tunnel in Europe. This and l'échelle de Fonserannes were the two keys to the construction of the canal. Along the way the canal is lined with plane trees, which were first planted during the Napoleonic Empire, and besides adding beauty, these give welcome shade from the hot Midi sun.

Unfortunately, many of them are now stricken with the canker stain, an incurable fungus, which slowly destroys the trees. The first outbreaks were observed in 2006 and it is now believed to have come from the wooden ammunition boxes brought to France during the Second World War by the United States Army. The North American trees were resistant to the fungus, but the French trees were not. Since then an aggressive campaign of selective tree removal in an attempt to stop the spread, but with poor results. The current consensus is that all forty-two thousand plane trees will need to be removed over a fifteen to twenty year period and replaced with fungus-resistant species.

About two-thirds of the way along the long pound, a branch canal leads off to the south fifteen kilometres through eleven locks into Narbonne. The mooring in the heart of the old city is across from the covered market and a short walk to the many museums. Narbonne was the most important city in the Roman Empire outside of Italy, and the city is crammed with museums and historic sites. There are many fine restaurants a short walk from the boat, but with the wonderful selection of fresh produce and fish from the nearby Mediterranean, a fine option is to play chef aboard and dine alfresco in your little patch of waterfront.

Back on le canal du Midi, the long pound finally ends and the locks begin again as the route wanders through wine country, with the vineyards of Minervois on the one bank and those of Corbières on the other. The canal passes through small towns and villages as it slowly makes its way up toward the pass. Many of these are well worth the pause to explore, but of particular interest is Carcassonne with its fortified hilltop La Cité. The site had been occupied since neolithic times and it was fortified by the Romans in the first century BC. The Romans ceded La Cité to the Visgoths in 462 and for the next thousand years and more, it was the target of attack by seemingly everyone with aspirations to power in Western Europe

The fortifications include a three-kilometre double wall with fifty-two towers. In 1849, because of their deteriorated state, the French government decided that the fortifications should be demolished. The locals strongly opposed this and a campaign was launched to preserve the fortress as an historical monument. The government reversed its decision, and in 1853 a restoration of La Cité was begun.

Canal Cruising in France

The cruise to the summit from Carcassonne passes through Castelnaudary, in the heart of the grain growing region of the Lauragais. The town is widely known as the origin of cassoulet, the baked casserole of white beans with duck or goose confit and pork sausages. The dish is the specialty through the region from Carcassonne to Toulouse, with recipe variations: Toulouse adds pork and mutton, while Carcassonne doubles the mutton and often replaces the duck with partridge. All variations are a very long way from the baked pork and beans of our youth, which are now more correctly called beans with pork fat. Cassoulet is well worth trying.

From Castelnaudary the canal ascends through two single locks, a triple lock and a double lock before arriving at Écluse Méditerranée, the final lock to the summit pound at 190 metres above sea level. This is one of the most gentle summit canals in France; the pass is rather flat and the pound runs for just over five kilometres before starting down toward the Atlantic. Near its western end is a fine place to stop to explore some of the seventeenth century works that supply water to the summit and upper locks on each side of it. There is a monument to Riquet, the builder of the canal.

Down through Écluse Océan begins the fifty kilometre passage to Toulouse and the end of le canal du Midi. The drop is only fifty-six metres, so the descent is gentle as it passes through

a mix of grain fields and forests with a light sprinkling of delightful small communities in which to pause to buy fresh baguettes and croissants, or to explore for a few hours, or to pause for lunch or for the day. This is very pleasant and gentle cruising country.

Because of the lack of quarried rock in the region, Riquet chose to use the local red Toulouse clay brick to build the humpbacked bridges here in the 1670s and 80s. During the Battle for Toulouse in 1814, toward the end of the Napoleonic Wars, the French army under Maréchal Sault ordered many of these bridges blown-up to cover the retreat of his troops from the British armies under the Duke of Wellington. The bridges were fully restored in 1821 and they remain in fine condition today and are still in regular use.

The city of Toulouse is at the end of le canal du Midi. At approximately 1.25 million people, it is the fourth largest metropolitan area in France after Paris, Lyon and Marseille. It is the centre of the European aerospace industry, with AirBus, the Galileo satellite positioning system, the SPOT satellite network and other associated companies. The site of the city was a key trading area between the Mediterranean, the Atlantic and the Pyrenees during the Iron Age and the settlement became a Roman military outpost in the second century BC. In the eight century it became the capital of Toulouse County in the Carolingian Empire and in 1271 it was incorporated into the Kingdom of France and began to establish itself as an artistic and intellectual city. Université de Toulouse was established in 1229 and the student population of the city is the third largest in France.

There are many things to see and do in Toulouse and the heart of the old city is an easy walk from Port St-Saveur, the mid-town marina. Medieval buildings line the narrow, winding streets in the centre of the old city and monumental public buildings surround squares, such as Place du Capitol. Musée des Augustins, a museum housed in a fourteenth century monastery, has splendid displays of paintings and sculptures and is worth a long visit. Displays in Musée Saint-Raymond are devoted to Antiquity and those in Musée de Toulouse focus on natural history.

Downstream five kilometres and through three locks from Port Saint-Saveur is the end of le canal du Midi. Here in a basin called l'Embouchoure is a three-way junction. The Canal du Midi leads in through the centre arch, and until 1843, barge traffic continued through a lock at the far end of the basin and down into the Garronne River for a tumultuous run in the current on the way downstream to Bordeaux. The arch on the right led to le canal de Brienne, a fifteen hundred metre canal that led barges to and from a lock into the Garonne River upstream of the weir for traffic upriver from Toulouse. The third arch was added in 1843 to give access to the newly completed Canal de Garonne, which made the barge voyage to Bordeaux much easier and safer.

Canal Cruising in France

Le canal de Garonne starts in the Midi-Pyrénées region in Toulouse, though much of it flows through the Aquitaine region and connects to other navigations there, so for continuity I will include its entire length here. Also the Lot River flows through the northern portion of the Midi-Pyrénées region before entering the Aquitaine and emptying into the Garonne River. Navigation on the lower Lot is in the Aquitaine, so to me it makes sense to also include the upper reaches near Cahors in this section.

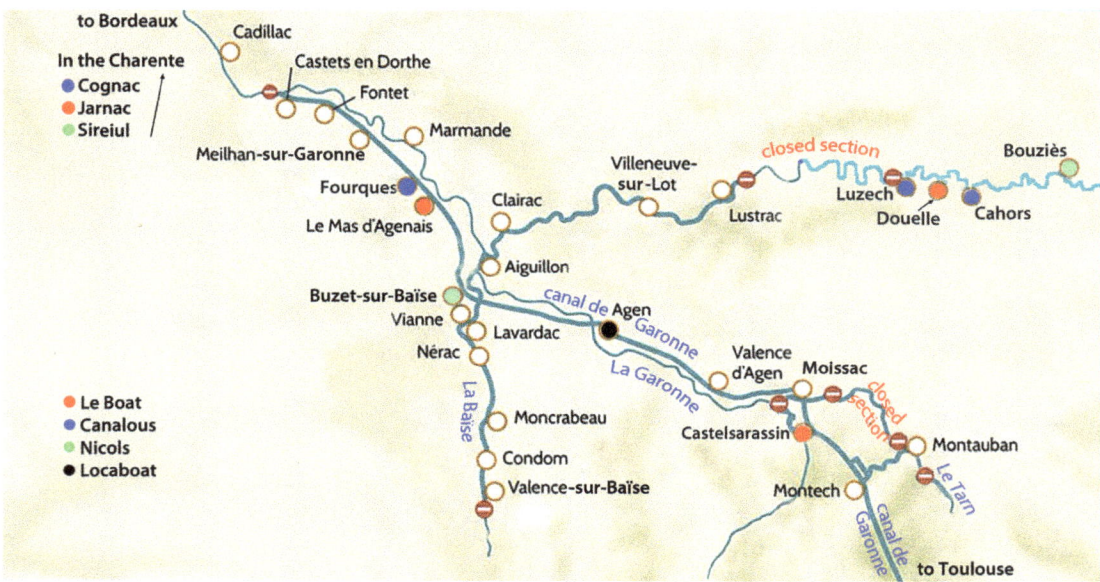

Branching off le canal de Garonne are five other navigation possibilities for rental boaters: the Canal de Montech, the Garonne River, the Tarn River, the Baïse River and the lower stretches of the Lot River. Navigation along the upper portion of the Lot River is not currently connected to the lower portion of the river, though work is in progress to restore the former navigation. It remains isolated from the remainder of the French waterways system. Also isolated from the contiguous system is the navigation along the Charente River in the Cognac area.

Among the four large rental companies there are twelve bases in the area; five are along le canal de Garonne, four are in the upper Lot River and three are along the Charente River. The only place in this area where a boat can be picked-up at one base and dropped off in another is between the Le Boat bases in Castelsarassin and Mas d'Agenais about 100 kilometres apart along le canal de Garonne. All other rentals require a retracing of the outbound route to return the boats.

From its beginning in Toulouse, le canal de Garonne runs through many kilometres of drab industrial areas, so it is obvious to see why the rental companies have not set-up here. After the end of the urban sprawl, the cruising becomes more relaxing and the scenery improves dramatically. By the time the canal arrives in Montech about forty kilometres from Toulouse, it has passed many pleasant towns and villages, either alongside the canal or a short distance away. The small town of Grisolles is a pleasant and welcoming stop.

At Montech is the junction with le canal de Montech, which leads through nine locks in its eleven kilometre descent to the Tarn River at Montauban. A pleasant walk along the Tarn River from le port de plaisance, the marina leads into the old city across its Pont Vieux, which was built at the beginning of the fourteenth century. The city of Montauban was founded in 1144 and it was one of the main bastions of Protestantism during the Religious Wars. Navigation along the Tarn River once allowed barges to travel the thirty-eight kilometres to Montauban from its junction with le Garonne, but the locks were closed in the mid twentieth century and navigation was discontinued. A movement is afoot to reopen the section.

Continuing down le canal de Garonne from Montech the canal steps down quickly through five locks in two kilometres. Alongside the series of locks is a water slope, which takes barges up and down the 13.3 metre elevation change. This structure was opened in 1974 and uses a motorized squeegee to move a wedge of water, which contains the barge, up and down a sloping concrete channel.

The city of Castelsarassin, a dozen kilometres along, dates to at least the mid-tenth century when it was named for the castle built in the Saracen era. The large marina is at the edge of the city centre, making it a convenient stop for shopping and explorations. Downstream, the canal crosses the Tarn River on an aqueduct before reaching Moissac.

Moissac is one of the finest places to stop along le canal de Garonne. The Tarn River flows past the city a hundred and fifty metres from the port, and there is a lock that takes boats up and down between the canal and the river. The Tarn is navigable here for a total of twelve kilometres: downstream to its junction with la Garonne and upstream to the first disused lock. Besides the moorings in the port, moorage is available in the quiet setting on the river next to a green park with easy access to the centre of the historic city.

Located in the city is one of the finest cloisters in France. There is reference to l'Abbaye de Moissac having been founded by Clovis I, King of France from 481 to 511, though modern scholars tend to attribute its founding to Dogbert's son, Clovis II, King of Burgundy and Neustria from 635 to 657. Whichever Clovis it was, the abbey goes back a long time. The construction of the Toulouse-Bordeaux railway through Moissac in 1845 destroyed much of the abbey, but fortunately the cloisters narrowly missed being destroyed. Today the cloisters and galleries are a UNESCO World Heritage Site.

They are magnificent. They surround a garth measuring twenty-seven by thirty-one metres, in one corner of which was once a large fountain fed by a spring in the adjacent hills. The gallery is supported by alternating single and double columns, each set with an intricately carved capital. There is a total of seventy-six of these capitals, each different from the others. The neighbouring abbey church, Église Saint-Pierre is also well worth a prolonged visit. It is famous for its sculpted south portal, created between 1115 and 1130. The stone carvings on the tympanum depict Saint John's vision of the Apocalypse. They were exquisitely rendered and remain in an excellent state of preservation.

Continuing from Moissac the canal threads its way through gentle countryside with huge orchards and vineyards along both sides. The vineyards specialize in the luscious Chasselas table grapes and the orchards are planted to plums, peaches and apples. There are pleasant towns along the way to in which to explore and restock before arriving in the city of Agen. The old city centre has much to see and in le musée des Beaux-Arts is a wide selection. Displays range from Palaeolithic, Bronze Age and Iron Age tools and artefacts through Gallo-Roman treasures and into paintings by Dutch masters and French Impressionists and many categories between.

Just outside Agen an aqueduct carries the canal over the Garonne River and a steep series of locks on the other side steps boats up and down from the plains beside the river. The canal continues through a small forest to a delightful stop at the town of Sérignac, which is notable for its old half-timbered houses and the twisted spire on its church. Continuing along past densely bushed canal banks and across an aqueduct over the Baïse River, the course leads to Buzet-sur-Baïse. This is the jumping-off point for explorations up the Baïse and the Lot Rivers.

A lock leads down from here to the Baïse River, which is subject to flooding when there are rains upstream. The lock keeper will not allow rental boaters down onto the river when it is in flood and port captains upstream at Nérac and Condom similarly control traffic. Most of the time the river is gentle with an easy to handle slow-moving current, but it can become a bit hairy during run-offs, particularly in the approaches to the narrow 4.15 metre locks. The navigable portion of the river is sixty-three kilometres long and there are twenty-one locks along the way.

The Baïse passes through the heart of the Armagnac region, famous for its fine brandy and there are several wonderful towns and cities to explore along its course. Nérac was a Gallo-Roman settlement though few vestiges of their occupation survive. The city is most famous as the birthplace and family home of Henry of Navarre Bourbon-Albret, who in 1589 became King Henry IV of France. Two centuries later, the family home, Château de Nérac, which dates to the fourteenth century, was near completely destroyed in the anti-royal fervour of the French Revolution. All that remains is one wing of the quadrangle, but it is huge and it now contains among other things, a museum.

The Among the other places worthy of a prolonged stop is Condom. Settlement in the area pre-dates the Romans and the city grew in prominence as a religious centre with the opening of its hôpital Saint-Jacques in 1314, it became an important stop on the pilgrimage to Saint Jacques de Compostela. There are many sites to visit in the city, including fourteenth and fifteenth century cathédrale Saint-Pierre de Condom, a fine example of Southern Gothic architecture. Beside the cathedral are wonderful cloisters that are now used as a public space. Well worth a visit nearby is the former Cistercian abbey, Notre-Dame de Flaran, which was founded in 1151 and is now a museum.

Ten kilometres upstream from Condom through the final three locks, we come to the end of navigation in the town of Valence-sur-Baïse. There is a large mooring basin below the town, which stands high on the escarpment behind fortified walls. Like many of the small towns in the region, the population has slowly declined, most of the shops have closed and the few remaining have limited hours.

From the lock at Buzet-sur-Baïse the river also leads downstream to its junction with the Garonne River. To descent the Garonne the five kilometres to the junction of the Lot River, a professional pilot is necessary. On a private boat with an experienced skipper and crew, the pilot drives the small piolt boat through the channel and the private boat follows. With a rental boat, the pilot comes aboard and drives the boat through the channel, often with the renting party being transported separately by boat or vehicle. The passage is made only when the river conditions are suitable. With levels too high, the current is too strong and with levels too low, there is insufficient water to get over the gravel banks.

It is well worth the effort to get into the Lot River; the scenery is beautiful and the cruising is relaxing. Above the second lock begins a long run of picture book settings; the mills at each end of the weir at Aguillon, the medieval buildings lining the winding streets of Clairac, and the incongruity of the Moorish architecture of the city hall in Castelmoron.

Above Castelmoron is a ten metre lock, but it is a very easy process locking through, since there are floating bollards in the walls which make the process simpler than doing the smaller locks with fixed bollards. Above this lock begins a broad and gentle twenty-eight kilometre pound to the next lock. All along the river on this stretch are many fine homes and castles both modern and ancient.

Along this pound is the ancient town of Caseneuil, which is at the junction of a small tributary. Lining the stream are ancient fortification walls that date back to the town's Roman foundation.

The decline of mining up river, combined by the increasing use of rail transportation, had caused le Lot River to be removed from the list of navigable waterways in 1926. Through the following decade large electric generating stations were built, with their dams flooding the old locks and weirs. In 1991 an isolated section of the river up and downstream of Cahors was reopened. In 1995 the lower 50 kilometres of the river from Aiguillon to Villeneuve-sur-Lot were restored to navigation. Downstream of Villeneuve-sur-Lot the passage goes through a gap in the old weir as it passes a decommissioned lock. The lock and lock house are now a thriving restaurant.

Shortly beyond here is wonderful old bridge across the river at Villeneuve-sur-Lot. This is a seventeenth century rebuild of the 1282 fortified bridge that had seen two of its arches washed away in floods. The two arches were replaced by one to ease the pressure of the flood currents and to make navigation safer. Above Villeneuve is a new thirteen metre high lock, which was opened through the dam in 2001, enabling another fifteen kilometres of navigation upstream.

Upstream, Saint-Sylvestre is a great stop, with a supermarket next to the mooring floats. Across the river and up on a hilltop is a wonderful fortified town, Penne d'Agenais. The town dates to the early thirteenth century, and hidden in a field beyond the pristinely manicured medieval buildings are the seemingly ignored ruins of the castle built by Richard the Lionheart, the future King Richard I of England.

Upstream from Saint-Sylvestre two of the old locks were restored to operation in 2010 to extend navigation to kilometre 75, the current end of navigation just below the next big hydroelectric dam at Lamothe. Work is in progress on linking the downstream 75 kilometres to the upstream section.

The first of these two locks, Écluse Lustrac is one of the prettiest lock settings on the French inland waterways. The old mill has been restored and converted into lofts and condominiums. At this point the river is entering a deeper valley with a wilder feel and a much reduced population. There are very few boats navigating the lower Lot River, possibly because of its remoteness and difficulty of access. Its beauty and history say there should be many more.

The Regions of France

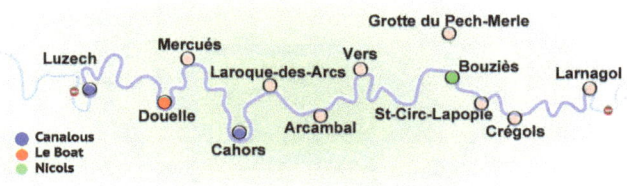

The upper reaches of the Lot River are disconnected from the remainder of the French inland navigation network, so boaters must access them by overland travel only. As we saw in the description of the lower reaches of the Lot River, this upper section, up and downstream of Cahors was reopened to navigation in 1991. It extends for seventy-five kilometres and three of the four major rental companies have bases here, either in or within a pleasant cruise of the city of Cahors, the capital of the Lot département.

Cahors has a long and diverse history including being a Celtic settlement before the Romans came in 50 BC. Its site is superbly defensive, being a narrow peninsula on a very sharp oxbow in the river. Construction on the fortified Pont Valentré, the symbol of the town, was began in 1308 and completed in 1378 to link the apex of the bend to the far bank. Around the city are the vineyards of Cahors, the famous 'black wine' that most accounts say pre-dates the wines of Bordeaux, with winemaking dating to the first Roman settlement.

The cuisine of the region is heavy with garlic, walnut oil, truffles, wild mushrooms and chestnuts. Corn-fed goose, duck and chicken as well as field raised lamb are common meats in roasts and casseroles. Foie gras, either mi-cuit or poélé is the regional speciality. Thankfully, it is hard to find bland food here.

The Lot River runs a sinuous course here as it cuts through sheer limestone escarpments. Perched on the rocks above the river are châteaux, such as Mercuès, Luzech and Cévenières, and clinging to the cliff sides are medieval villages like St-Cyrc-Lapopie, Clavignac and La Toulzanie. Some of the most beautiful cruising scenery in France is along the upper reaches of the Lot. The area has been settled and populated since prehistory and throughout there are traces dating back tens of thousands of years.

At Cabrerets about two kilometres north of the river is the prehistoric cave of Pech Merle. The area is also easily accessed by road from Cahors in about half an hour. It is one of the few prehistoric cave painting sites in France that remains open to the general public. The cave extends far back into the rock through an ancient stream course. About a kilometre and a half from the entrance are large caverns with walls painted in dramatic murals dating from the Gravettian culture some 22,000 to 32,000 years ago. Visitors are limited to 700 per day to preserve the paintings, so in high season, reservations are strongly recommended.

The tiny village of Saint-Cyrc-Lapopie has been called the most beautiful village in France. It clings precariously to the cliffs high above a gorge at a bend in the river, and is thought to have first been sited there for defensive purposes during Gallo-Roman times. In medieval times it was one of the stops on the Pilgrimage of Saint-Jacques de Compostela Today there are about two hundred residents in the village, many involved in serving the 400,000 visitors each year, which is an average of more than a thousand per day. In the tiny village are at least ten restaurants and a number of bars and cafés, as well as many souvenir shops.

All along the navigable length of the upper Lot are so many small towns and villages each with their own beauty, charm and uniqueness, that they seem commonplace. If any one of them were transported to another region of the country, it would be a major attraction, but here they are just a part of the scenery to be enjoyed while cruising the Lot.

The other cruising destination in the region is the Charente River north of Bordeaux. The river was closed to navigation in the mid-twentieth century and the locks were abandoned, but they have recently been restored for navigation. The Charente is now open through twenty-one locks from its mouth at Port-des-Barques on the Atlantic coast to Angoulême 164 kilometres upstream The lower forty-eight kilometre stretch of the river is free flowing and tidal from the lock at Saint-Savenin to the sea. There are large marinas in Rochefort, and there is very little reason to head downstream through increasing tidal current the final twenty kilometres from there to the mouth.

Upstream of the Saint-Savenin lock the river takes on its gentle and clear watered nature. With only two locks in the next fifty-seven kilometres to the city of Cognac, the river flows through a gently rolling countryside of vineyards, meadows and pine woods. The terrain becomes more hilly beyond Cognac and in the fifty-nine kilometres from there to Angoulême there are eighteen locks. Because the Charente River is isolated from the remainder of the French network, there is no traffic other than locals and renters.

The Charente passes through the heart of the Cognac growing, distilling and aging region, which for centuries has been producing the world's most famous brandy.

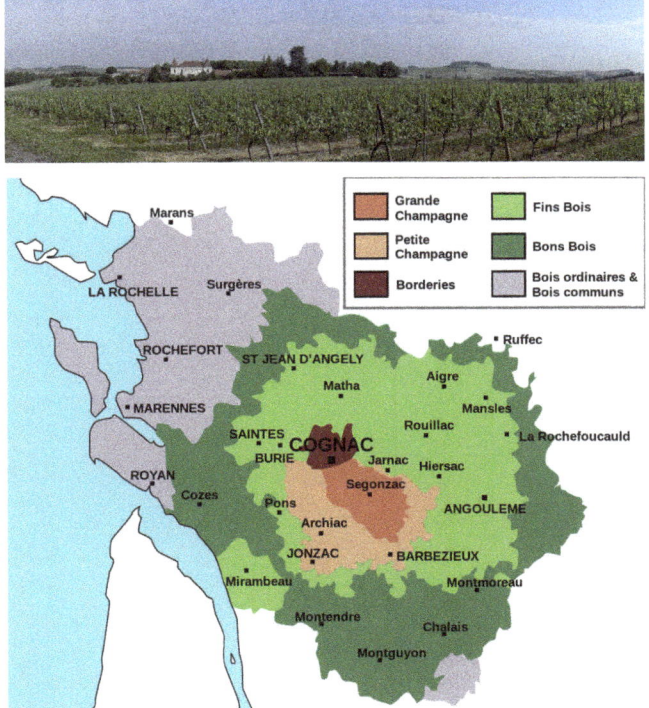

The difference in soil structure across the region makes brandies of differing character and quality. The small central regions near the cities of Cognac and Jarnac, are characterized by shallow clay-limestone soil over beds of limestone and chalk. These produce distillates of the most desirable quality and are used in the finest blends. The acetic white wine made from Ugni Blanc grapes is double distilled in large copper alembics of regulated size and then aged for a minimum of two years in Limousin oak casks. Throughout the region are vast warehouses of aging brandy, which during the first few years looses about three percent of its volume per year through evaporation of the water and alcohol. This is called the 'angel's share'.

The four largest producers: Courvoisier, Hennessy, Martell and Rémy Martin, are owned by major international conglomerates. All of them, as well as many of the smaller houses offer tours and tastings, most with a small fee. Reservations are recommended and can be very easily made online.

But the region is much more than just brandy. There is history and culture dating back into antiquity. The city of Saintes was the Roman capital of the Aquitaine and many Roman structures remain there, such as the triumphal arch of Germanicus built near the beginning of the first century, and the large amphitheatre built into a hillside during the first half of the first century.

In the cities of Cognac, Jarnac and Angoulême, there are long wharves where casks of Cognac were once loaded onto barges for transportation to aging chais, to blending rooms or to market. The barges are gone now, except for a few that operate tourist excursions along the river, so finding a place to moor is rather easy.

At the head of navigation is the city of Angoulêm, built on a plateau overlooking a meander of the Charente River. It dates back beyond the Roman settlement there two thousand years ago and was later fortified and became a strategic position at the centre of many roads, highly coveted and suffering many sieges. Its tumultuous past has build a depth of historical, religious, and urban heritage making it an intriguing place to visit.

The twenty-one locks along the river are manual and self-operated, so unlike systems in most of the other parts of France, the locks do not close for lunch. The cruising follows a very relaxed, and unscheduled pace.

The final cruising region is located in the northeast corner of France in Brittany and Pays de la Loire, each a separate political region. Their navigations are linked to each other by an eighty-five kilometre section of the Loire River, but the channel is constantly shifting, so passage requires local knowledge and a skilled skipper. Because of this, the rental companies do not allow their boats to use it. Essentially, for renters the boating areas of Brittany and Maine-Anjou are disconnected from each other. Additionally, the entire area is disconnected from the remainder of the French inland waterways system, making the main traffic the rental boats and the locals plus an occasional cruiser that approaches the system from the sea.

Each of the four major companies offers boats in Brittany, with all but Locaboat having at least two bases. There are four main waterways here, the first, Canal d'Ille et Rance cuts across the peninsula of Brittany using forty-eight locks in its eighty-five kilometres from the end of the tidal Rance upstream of Saint-Malo on the English Channel to Rennes, where it meets the Vilaine River. The second

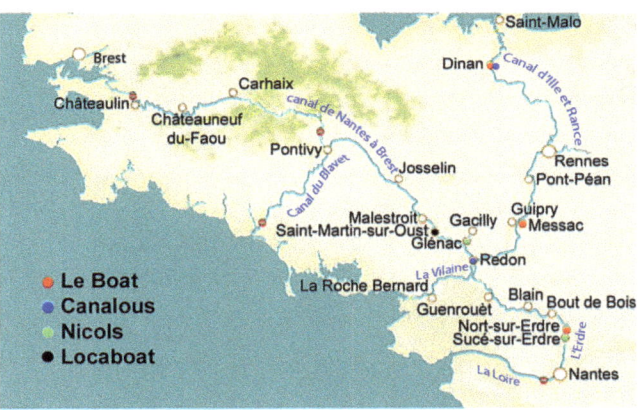

waterway is the Vilaine River, which leads down from Rennes through thirteen locks in one hundred thirty kilometres to the lock into the Atlantic below La Roche Bernard.

The Vilaine River is crossed at Redon by the third waterway, canal de Nantes à Brest. This canal was the inspiration of Napoleon around the time of the Battle of Trafalgar in 1805, conceived as route to circumvent possible English blockades of sea routes from Nantes on the Loire to the strategic port of Brest at the tip of Brittany. The canal finally opened in 1842, and at 365 kilometres in length and 238 locks, it was the longest canal in France. A hydroelectric dam at Guerlédan in the 1920s interrupted the canal and there is now an eighty kilometre gap. The seventy-six kilometre western portion is navigable, but bereft of rental boat bases. The central portion from Pontivy to Redon and the eastern portion from Redon to Nantes are restored to navigation along their 206 kilometres. The fourth waterway runs from Pontivy. Another of Napoleon's inspirations, canal du Blavet leads seventy kilometres down through twenty-eight locks to another strategic port, L'Orient. These waterways are well served by rental bases.

Archaeologists have found traces including a fire hearth indicating that Brittany was populated by Neanderthals as far back as 450,000 years ago. In much more modern times, it was settled by Celts from the north and then occupied by the Romans when it became part of the Roman Republic in 51 BC. During the late fourth century immigration of Britons began and increased the following century as the Anglo-Saxon invaded Britain. Early in the tenth century invasions by Vikings took large pieces of territory, including Normandy and Anjou to the east.

The Vikings were expelled forty years later and the Kingdom of Brittany became a Duchy with allegiance to France. Through marriage and succession, Brittany was absorbed as a province of France in 1532, but the Bretons maintained their fierce independent spirit. The French language was not widely spoken until the nineteenth century, the locals preferring their traditional Breton or Gallo. French is now the official language and is almost universally spoken.

The Brittany region is as complex as its history. There is so much to see and do that a short trip cannot get it all in and visitors will want to remain longer. The crisp white Muscadet wines from the vineyards along the Loire Valley near Nantes are a perfect match for the fish and shellfish of the area. The traditional drink of Brittany, however, is its cider and this goes well with the iconic savoury buckwheat galettes of the region. Among other traditional Breton dishes are the sweet butter crêpes that are eaten as dessert.

In the Maine-Anjou area of the Loire only Canalous and Niclols have bases. Because of shifting shallow shoals, rental boats are not permitted to navigate on the Loire River here. The permitted navigation is along 134 kilometres of the Sarthe River with twenty locks from Angers northeastward to Le Mans. Northward from Angers, the Mayenne River leads 123 kilometres through forty-five locks to Mayenne. Along the way there is an eighteen kilometre branching with three locks up the Oudon River. The rental bases are distributed to make it easy to explore all these waterways.

Besides being King Henry II of England from 1154 to 1189, Henry Plantagenet was also Count of Anjou, Maine and Nantes, Duke of Normandy and Aquitaine and Lord of Ireland. He also at various times controlled Wales, Scotland and Brittany. In 1205 Anjou was seized from the English by the King Philip II of France and made a Duchy, which it remained until the French Revolution, so the region has a long French tradition.

The lower reaches of both the Sarthe and the Mayenne rivers flow through the Anjou vineyards and along the way there are many opportunities to visit, tour and taste. Though there are great Anjou wines, this is the generic Anjou area, where the wines are mostly inexpensive and uncomplicated. They are made as reds, rosés and whites in styles from dry to sweet and offer good value.

The city of Angers demands a thorough visit, with many things to see and explore, such as the thirteenth century château des ducs d'Anjou and le cathédrale Saint-Maurice, which was built as a transition between Romanesque and Gothic style. Up the Sarthe River are many more wonderful displays of architecture, like Château Plessis-Bourré north of Cheffes sur Sarthe. Visitors are welcomed at this moated castle.

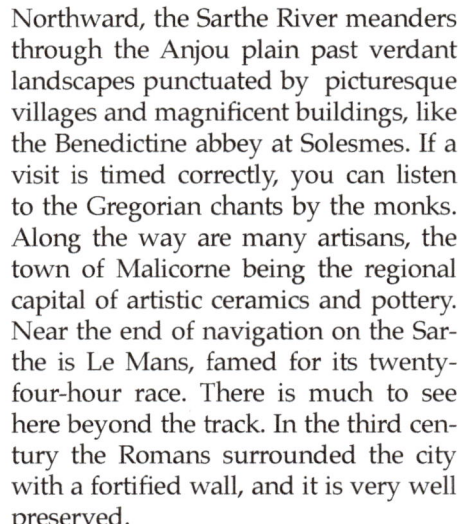

Northward, the Sarthe River meanders through the Anjou plain past verdant landscapes punctuated by picturesque villages and magnificent buildings, like the Benedictine abbey at Solesmes. If a visit is timed correctly, you can listen to the Gregorian chants by the monks. Along the way are many artisans, the town of Malicorne being the regional capital of artistic ceramics and pottery. Near the end of navigation on the Sarthe is Le Mans, famed for its twenty-four-hour race. There is much to see here beyond the track. In the third century the Romans surrounded the city with a fortified wall, and it is very well preserved.

Following the Mayenne River and its branch, the Oudon, takes boaters through peaceful landscapes and past amazing heritage. There are old mills with their waterwheels, quaint little villages, towns with ancient churches and much more. Laval is the major city along the river and is a delightful place to stop and experience. The oldest streets and buildings, dating back to Middle Ages, are around the promontory on which Château de Laval stands. This old core is today the main shopping area, with several pedestrian streets with little shops and medieval half-timbered houses.

This concludes our clockwise circuit of the main inland cruising areas of France. In it, I have lightly touched on a few highlights from each of the regions in an attempt to give the reader a sense of their background, flavour and character. Each of the regions is quite different from the others, just as each bend of a river or canal leads to a different setting.

Chapter Three

Historic French Barges

The English word barge traces its origin to 1300 from the Old French, which had adopted it from colloquial Latin. The word originally referred to any small boat and the modern meaning didn't evolve until around 1480. The word bark, meaning a small ship, entered the English language around 1420 from the Old French word barque, which had come from the colloquial Latin barca at the beginning of the fifth century. By the seventeenth century, the word bark was being used to refer to a three-masted ship, and it often used the French spelling, barque to distinguish this meaning. Both colloquial Latin words had likely evolved from the classic Latin barica and from the Greek baris, meaning Egyptian boat. The Coptic word bari meant small boat. The Ancient Egyptian word ba-y-r, hieroglyphic ⛵ referred to a basket-shaped boat.

In the context used in this book, a barge is a flat-bottomed vessel of shallow draft that was designed for navigation along a river or canal. They evolved differently in each region, their designs dictated by local navigational conditions and the nature of the cargoes they carried.

Throughout the Middle Ages in France, most of the heavy inland transportation was along the courses of its many rivers. Shallow boats of simple design and construction drifted and sailed downstream with the current and were sailed, pulled or poled back up. Often, where the current was too strong for the upstream voyage, crude barges were cheaply built to last only the downstream trip. On arrival with their cargo, they were broken-up and sold as lumber or firewood.

Different regional uses spawned dozens of designs, such as: the marnois of the Marne, upper Seine and Yonne valleys; the chaland from the Loire; the sisselande from the Saône and Rhône; the courpet in the Dordogne; the chalibardon on the Adour; and the sapine of the Allier. Very few examples of these have survived, but in recent years enthusiasts have built working replicas of some of the old designs.

Two Chalands unloading at Orléans on the Loire

With the coming of the canals, barge designs quickly evolved to take advantage of the still waters made possible by the locks. The barges grew in length and width to match the dimensions of the locks and bridge cuts they needed to transit. Their draft increased to the maximum depth available on the canal. In many regions of France, cargo barges became rather boxy in appearance, but there were exceptions.

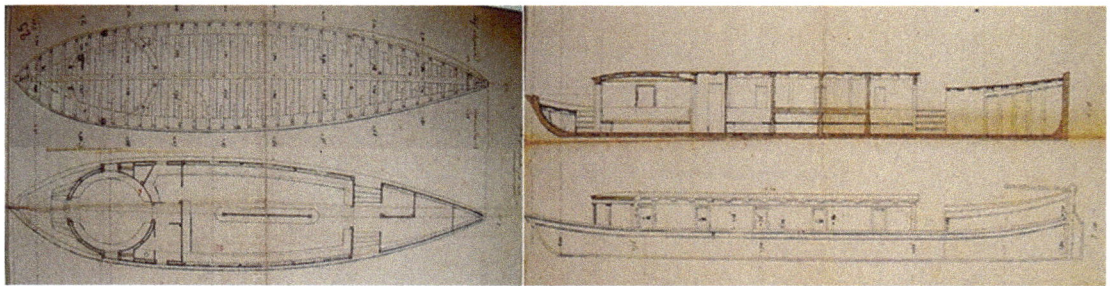

With the 1681 opening of le canal royal en Languedoc, (now called le Canal du Midi), the demand for fast passenger service was quickly met. Post boats were designed and built for the opening and they began providing a fast, efficient transportation system between Toulouse and Agde.

To save time spent in locks, a total of forty boats shuttled in the pounds between the locks and passengers changed boats at the ends of the pounds. Fresh horses at the trot hauled the post boats along at eight kilometres per hour in vessels that could accommodate fifty passengers, divided between the first class lounge in the front and the communal room in the centre. Passengers took their beds and meals ashore in the hostels along the canal, while the helmsman had accommodations in the vessel's stern.

The 240 kilometre journey from Toulouse to Agde took four days. Boat designs and management of the system evolved and by 1834 the boats were travelling at ten kilometres per hour and the

trip was cut to three days. With later canal construction, the service expanded to Beaucaire on the Rhône and Agen on the Garonne upstream from Bordeaux. At its peak, the passenger volume reached 100,000 per year. In 1858 the opening of the railway almost immediately killed the post boat service; it didn't quite make two centuries.

Sailing was one of the methods of propelling a barge along a river or canal, but in vessels with flat bottoms and little or no keel, this was limited to downwind sailing. In contrary winds, the barge had to either be poled or hauled. The current in the lower 400 kilometres of the Loire flows to the west and the prevailing wind blows upstream from the west. This enabled barges to run downstream with the current and sail back up in a following wind.

In canals and rivers with no current or gentle currents and few favourable winds, hauling was done by men. With family operated barges, often the women and children would do the hauling, while the man tended to more exacting tasks like relaxing, smoking and steering. It takes some effort to get the barge moving, but in calm conditions, little effort is required to keep it moving at two kilometres per hour.

More often in France, horses were used, and sometimes oxen. Moving along at six kilometres per hour through the placid waters of a canal pound in this fashion was peaceful. Towpaths had been built alongside the canals and through the bridge cuts and the only complications were when meeting a barge coming in the opposite direction. Tow lines had to be detached from harnesses and reattached once the barges had drifted past each other.

Canal Cruising in France

On rivers with stronger currents, such as the Saône and the Rhône, barges like the sisselande were steered using long sweep oars. For better control when heading downstream in swift current, they often used steering sweeps both fore and aft.

To make the re-ascent against the current required very large teams of horses. Depending on the current, this could mean from twenty to as many as forty horses, and these required one driver for every two or three horses.

Animal haulage along the faster moving sections of the Saône and the Rhône quickly diminished around 1840 with the expanding use of steam tugs. In a few hours these powerful new machines could haul a long string of barges upstream through the current over a distance that would have required two hundred horses and seventy to one hundred men a day or more to accomplish. The Industrial Revolution was in full swing.

On the more gentle rivers and on many of the canals, less powerful steam tugs began being used to pull long trains of barges. In much of Western Europe there was a ready adoption of these new methods, though an exception to this was in France, where the old ways, the gentle and quiet ways were maintained by many.

Motorized tractors began appearing on the towpaths to replace animals. Various versions were also devised of electric motors running suspended from overhead cables.

In some of areas, such as Cambrai, rail-mounted traction machines were introduced. Then in 1926 la Compagnie Générale de Traction sur les Voies Navigables (CGTVN) was established in the north and east of France. The company operated electric tractors running on rails on the towpaths. The transition to the mechanical haulage was resisted by bargemen, many of whom saw it as a disruption to their gentle ways.

However, the traditional barge operators were being challenged on another front. Since the turn of the century, engines had begun being installed in barges. Initially this was usually a retrofit to an existing wooden barge, but gradually new iron or steel barges, loosely called automoteurs, were designed specifically for power. However, unlike in other areas of Europe, the transition to motor barges in France was slow.

In 1935 there were still 1500 working bateaux-écurie, horse barges along the French canals. Most of these were built of wood and they were equipped with horse stables and a loading ramp to move the horses between the barge and the bank. By the late 1950s horse haulage was still common along the canals, but the horses were being gradually re-

placed by electric traction along the towpaths. The northern and eastern canals were the first to retire horses, but in the centre of France, horses stayed on despite the powered tractors and the convenience of powered barges. The last bateau-écurie docked in 1969. The self-powered barges gradually took over, and because of a lack of business, in 1972 la Compagnie Générale de Traction sur les Voies Navigables filed for bankruptcy.

The style of barge most common in France in the late nineteenth century and through the first half of the twentieth was the péniche, which was based on the Flemish Spits. This 1908 photo, taken during a chomage, when the canal was drained for maintenance, shows its boxy shape.

The standard péniche had evolved to take full advantage of the maximum space available in the canal locks. The new gauge for canals that was implemented in 1879 by the French Minister of Transport, Charles-Louis Freycinet, had been based on the péniche dimensions.

At the end of the nineteenth century there were about 12,000 commercial canal boats in France. Of these, 8000 were the péniches in northern France that were employed with hauling coal to Paris.

The péniche was based on the Flemish spits, which the French called bélandre, It had evolved from the Dutch bijlander, whose name meaning near land, referred to its coastal use. Its gracefully curved ends, sweeping sheer and tumblehome bulwarks were the results of how wood could be bent in building a ship's hull.

That such a graceful ship as the bijlander had evolved in Belgium and France into the mundane, utilitarian péniche, is a major reason why modern canal boating enthusiasts gravitate to Dutch barges.

Chapter Four

Historic Dutch Barges

The geography and conditions in the Netherlands caused inland boats to evolve very differently from those in France. The bijlander, from which the French bélandre and then the péniche had descended, was a flat-bottomed vessel used for coastal trade. Variations of it are known back to about 1500.

From the bijlander the tjalk evolved in the seventeenth century. Tjalk is a rather generic term used to designate a long, narrow and shallow barge shaped somewhat like a shoebox with rounded corners. Most tjalks had a mast rigged with a gaff, they carried a bowsprit, and because of the shallow waters of the Netherlands, they had flat bottoms and no keel. To counter the press of the wind when sailing, they were fitted with leeboards. Their gracefully rounded ends and pronounced sheer lead to their being likened to Dutch wooden shoes.

There were many different styles of tjalk, their variations being based on the particular conditions and intended uses where they were built and sailed. They were broadly classified by style, such

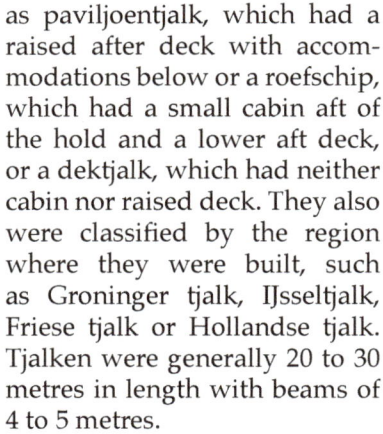

as paviljoentjalk, which had a raised after deck with accommodations below or a roefschip, which had a small cabin aft of the hold and a lower aft deck, or a dektjalk, which had neither cabin nor raised deck. They also were classified by the region where they were built, such as Groninger tjalk, IJsseltjalk, Friese tjalk or Hollandse tjalk. Tjalken were generally 20 to 30 metres in length with beams of 4 to 5 metres.

The skûtsje was a smaller tjalk, shorter and narrower to trade in the shallow lakes and narrow, winding canals in southwest Friesland. They were generally between 15 and 20 metres in length and had beams 3.4 to 4 metres. The skûtsje was developed between 1855 and 1860 and they were initially built of wood. Then in 1887 riveted iron was introduced, and during the first decade of the twentieth century, the yards gradually converted from iron to steel. A total of 870 iron and steel skûtsjes were built until the final one in 1933.

With the closing of the Zuiderzee in 1932, the commercial usefulness of the skûtsje dropped. Some had engines fitted, but even then, they could not compete with the purpose-built motor barges. During the ensuing years, many skûtsjes were scrapped, some were converted to homes and some to pleasure or racing vessels. There are currently about 90 of these historic vessels restored to full sailing trim and competing in regular races in Friesland.

The larger tjalken also declined in usefulness as the new breed of motor barges took over the commerce. Like the skûtsje, many were scrapped, but hundreds of them have survived. Many live on as woonboten, houseboats permanently moored along the canals, while others have been converted for pleasure cruising. In most towns around the IJsselmeer there are restored sailing tjalken offering a variety of trips, tours and charters.

Other unpowered sailing barges included various versions of the aak, such as the Hasselteraak, Lemsteraak, boeieraak, and klipperaak. Like the tjalk, these had leeboards for sailing. With their hulls not designed for motor propulsion, they too became commercially obsolete and other uses were found for them. Unfortunately, for many, this meant the scrap heaps.

In the early 1920s the old non-motorized barges became uncompetitive after the introduction of the luxemotor, the modern classic of Dutch ship design. Its sharp, plumb entry and its stern designed for proper water flow to the propeller made it an efficient and fast barge. Adding to its attraction and giving the barge its name were the luxurious accommodations in the stern.

With their larger hold capacity, much better efficiency and greater comfort, luxemotors quickly became the standard on the canals of the Netherlands, rapidly replacing the older aak and tjalk hull styles. They were built in lengths from 18 to 30 metres, though many were lengthened in the 1950s in an attempt to compete with the falling price of truck freight. Even with lengthening, the design became increasingly commercially unviable in face of competition from more modern barges.

Other types of motor barge enjoyed some limited success during the reign of the luxemotor. The steilesteven, with a fatter stern and its wheelhouse all the way aft, provided an increased hold capacity. Another was the kitwijker, which like the steilsteven was designed originally without an engine. Neither ever achieved the popularity of the luxemotor, and they too were eclipsed by improved designs after the middle of the twentieth century.

Retired examples of the luxemotor, the stilesteven and the kitwijker are also popular choices for makeover to liveaboard and cruising barges. With the tjalks and aaks, they form the most popular group of barges for conversion to pleasure cruising on the canals of Europe.

Chapter Five

Pleasure Cruising in France

I first became aware of the European canals in 1966 while I was serving in France with the Royal Canadian Air Force. In the Lorraine, the Champagne, the Franche Comté and the Burgundy I saw old brown péniches moving slowly along the canals, I watched some of the last horse haulage on the towpaths and I frequently paused to watch barges passing through locks. I saw no pleasure boating.

After I had resigned my commission from the Royal Canadian Navy in 1981, I set-up in the wine business. For two decades we made very frequent visits to Europe while searching for wines to import or later while conducting wine and food tours. During these trips we always spent a week or two or longer in France and never failed to search-out the canals and watch the activity along them.

In 1984 we rented our first canal boat in France from Blue Line in St-Jean-de-Losne in the Burgundy. It was mid-spring and we had le canal de Bourgogne, le canal du Centre and le Saône almost completely to ourselves. There was minimal commercial traffic, it was off-season for the few hotel barges that existed at the time and we saw very few other rental boats and even fewer private cruisers during our three weeks. The lock houses on the canals all had resident lock keepers, with whom we paused to chat while assisting them with the gates and sluices. We bought fresh eggs and garden produce from them and learned of interesting places to visit and favourite dining spots. We were hooked.

I had not been able to find a travel agent in Canada with any knowledge of French canal boat rentals, so I had to write to Blake's in England to book our boat. Since then the number of companies offering canal boat rentals rapidly increased and then slowly declined. There are currently four large national companies with bases throughout France and forty-three smaller regional companies with one or a few bases each. Together they offer canal boat fleets in every navigable area of France. The boat rental business is an important and consolidating tourism sector.

The latest Voies Navigables de France (VNF) report dated 2013 shows that the four large national companies have 1132 boats and that the next three largest operators have a total of only 100 boats among them. The remaining forty companies operate the remaining 372 boats. The average number of beds across the entire rental fleet has increased from 5.6 per boat in 2003 to 6.6 per boat in 2012, showing an adjustment and rationalization of the floating inventory.

Pleasure Cruising in France

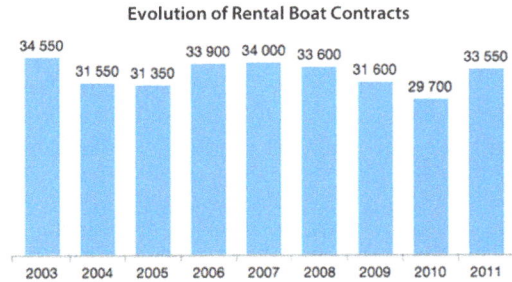
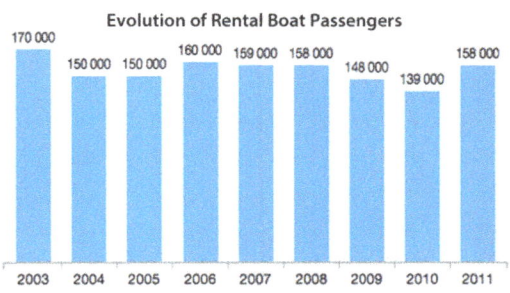

The latest VNF report shows that these forty-seven rental companies offer a total of 1604 boats from 121 rental bases throughout France. These numbers are down from 1911 boats and 125 bases in 2003; however, while the number of boats has declined by sixteen percent, the number of rental contracts has fallen by less then three percent, showing a consolidation of the rental fleet and a better use of it. Similarly, the number of passengers per year has declined by only seven percent. Precipitating these was the world financial crisis of 2008-09, which tipped the trend downward, as did the decline of travel in the post 11 November 2001 environment.

One of the great attractions of the rental boats is that they require no boating experience or knowledge, no boating skills or training, no license or qualifications to operate. A brief introduction to the operation of the boat is given at the beginning of the rental period, but effectively, with very little boating awareness, most renters are set free to learn boat handling for themselves. The 2013 VNF report states that almost fifty percent of the rental activity is in the south and southwest and that seventy-two percent of the rentals are for a week or less.

In 2014, a typical weekly rental fee for a boat for two people was €1300 in low season, around €1700 in shoulder season and close to €2000 in high season. This Dutch-built Linssen 28 Sedan is a fine example of a two-person rental boat.

Larger boats for four, six, eight, ten and more people cost more, but the small incremental increase per additional bed makes multi-couple rentals very popular. A 14.9-metre boat like the Linssen Euroclassic 149 shown here, with four cabins all with ensuite showers and toilets rents for €2700, €3300 and €3750 in low, shoulder and high seasons, about half the rate per person than for the smaller boat.

Another popular way to cruise the canals is aboard a hotel barge. Though a few were purpose-built, most are converted freight or general cargo barges, gutted and refitted with high-quality interiors. There are currently seventy-six hotel barges in France with a total of more than a thousand guest beds. They range greatly in size, accommodating from four to twenty-four guests and they also vary in the quality of the accommodations, amenities and dining provided. Most are fully catered and have organized tours and activities ashore as the barges slowly cruise their itineraries along the canals.

Many of the largest ones are converted péniches or spits and among the smaller hotel barges are converted tjalken, aaken and luxemotors. A common feature is a high staff-to-guest ratio, with the smaller barges often providing higher comfort and individual attention. Weekly rates generally run in the €3000 to €4000 per person range. Some barges with more basic accommodation and self-catering cost under €2000 per person, but for a grande luxe hotel barge, the weekly rates are around €5000 per person.

Most of the hotel barges follow a set itinerary throughout the season, doing a cruise in one direction along the canal one week and retracing the route in the opposite direction the next. A few are more pelagic, their itinerary being along a canal or series of canals with guests joining in one location and disembarking at the end of the week in another as the barge works its way through one or more regions. Some of the smaller barges are known to write their itineraries based where their early-booking clients want to explore and then connect the dots and fill-in the gaps with later bookings.

River cruises form another category of inland pleasure cruising. In recent years the popularity of cruises on the Rhône and Saône has rapidly increased. In the latest report sixteen operators were running thirty-eight river cruise ships with a total 4976 passenger beds and they carried a total of 222,850 passengers for 910,900 nights, up more than ten percent in a year. Many of river cruise itineraries are week long; however, there are also three, four and five day itineraries. Most of the prices are in the range of €90 to €150 per person per night, though some are much higher,.

Pleasure Cruising in France

Not mentioned in the VNF report were the privately owned and operated pleasure boats, though according to other VNF figures, there are currently over 20,000 active private boats on the inland waterways of France, fifty percent of which are foreign owned. This private fleet is nearly ten times the size of the entire commercial pleasure fleet, but its impact on the economy is considerably less, providing an average of less than €5000 per boat, compared to the €190,000 average per commercial boat. Because of this, private boats receive very little support with infrastructure and facilities.

However; owning one's own vessel on the waterways offers the most freedom and flexibility. In 2000 I bought my first canal boat in France. Lady Jane was a 14-metre Dutch motorkruiser built of steel in Groningen in 1970. After a refurbishing refit, we cruised throughout northeastern France on the Saône, the Canal du Rhône à Rhin, the Canal du Centre, the Canal de Bourgogne. We wandered up through the Franche-Comté, crossed into the Champagne, spent time in Paris, explored the upper Seine, the Yonne, Loing, the Briare and the Loire.

After six years on the French canals, I grew restless and wanted some wild and remote sailing. While I was still young enough, I wanted to sail through Patagonia and around Cape Horn. I sold Lady Jane and had a new 15-metre cutter-rigged sloop built and in 2009 we sailed south from Vancouver. After three years exploring South America, we rounded Cape Horn and headed up the Atlantic. Along the way, in dealing with stultifying bureaucracies, sparse resources and a hurricane and three Force 11 storms at sea, we realized that we were approaching our best-before-dates for wild cruising. We headed back to Europe and bought another canal boat, this one a 1908 Dutch barge and we are again enjoying a more sedate and gentle style of boating.

Chapter Six

A Look at the Rental Boats

Owning one's own cruiser or barge on the French canals is a dream many share; however, the limitations of finances, the requirements for certification and licensing, the constraints of time, the pressures of earning a living and the commitment to raising a family prevent the vast majority of people from realizing this dream. Notwithstanding all of these hurdles, the pleasures of cruising along the French waterways can be experienced by rental boat with no commitment, and for boats under fifteen metres in length, no training, no certification and no boating skills.

As we have seen in Chapter Two, Ftance has a broad variety of cruising areas from which to chose. This broad variety carries on into the selection of a rental boat; there is a very wide range of style, size, and level of comfort available. Each of the four national rental companies offer boats to suit from two people on up to groups of ten or more. Most of the sizes in this range come in a differing levels of comfort, from basic to luxurious. The bulk of the offerings are in four, six or eight bed sizes. The four bed, two cabin models are stated as suitable for a couple with two children or for two couples, the six bed, three cabin models are comfortable for six singles, three couples, two couples with two children, and so on up the size scale.

As we saw in the VNF report in the previous chapter, the average rental boat in France now has 6.6 beds, up one bed from a decade earlier. This indicates either that renters want more space, or that they are renting in larger groups. From what we have seen the past couple of years of cruising through the Burgundy, the Midi and the Aquitaine, larger rental boats with large groups of people aboard is more common now than I remember from ten and fifteen years ago.

One of the common pieces of terminology used in describing a boat's accommodation is the 'sleeps 6 +2', 'sleeps 8 +2' or 'sleeps 10 +2'. While in some boat configurations, this means that there are fold-down pullman beds in a couple of the cabins to convert them from two to three beds, more often the term means that the extra two sleeping spaces are made-up by rearranging cushions on the salon settee or converting the dinette into a double bed.

Except in the budget category, it is common to have en-suite washrooms with the cabins. Also, many of the beds can be configured either as a double or as two singles to accommodate the sleeping preferences of the broadest range of rental parties. Most boats are equipped for comfortable cruising with fully equipped galleys (the nautical term for kitchen) with fridge, gas oven, stove top, hot and cold running water, pots, pans and utensils, dishes, cutlery and glasses. Bed linen, bath towels and tea towels are not always included, so you may need to bring or to rent these to set-up comfortable housekeeping.

Canal Cruising in France

In the following pages we will take a look at representative boats from each of the four national rental companies: Le Boat, Canalous, Nicols and Locaboat.

 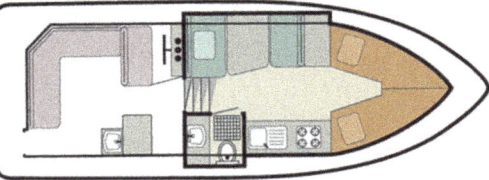

Le Boat offers a full range of boats, currently with more than forty different models to accommodate from two to twelve people. These range from basic comfort through luxurious. At the bottom of the scale of their offerings is the Capri TS, a 9 metre long boat with a beam of 3.2 metres. Listed as sleeping two or three and is laid-out with one cabin with a double bed and a love seat in the saloon that converts into single bed. It has a single washroom with an integral shower and it comes with basic comforts, including an electric refrigerator and a gas cooktop, an oven and a grill. The steering position is protected from the elements and has good visibility, and there's easy access to the outside deck.

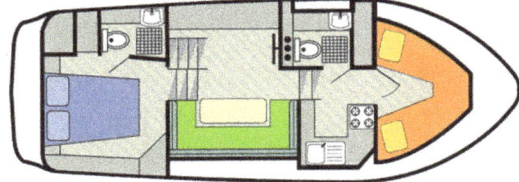

In the middle of the range in both size and comfort is the Countess 4+2. This boat is 10.2 metres in length and 3.56 metres wide and has two cabins. . The forward cabin has two single beds with an adjacent shower and toilet and is ideal for children or two adults. The aft cabin is a very private stateroom with a double bed and an en-suite shower and toilet.

There is an inside steering station in the central salon and across from it is a settee that converts into a double bed, taking maximum accommodation to six. The U-shaped galley has an electric refrigerator, a cook top a sink and plenty of cabinet space. The interior is well laid-out, giving a sense of roominess and the living space spreads to the rear deck, where there is a second helm position and is an ideal venue for socialising and watching the scenery glide by.

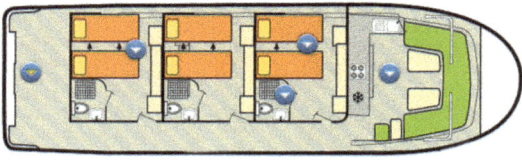

At the luxurious end of the scale, Le Boat's Vision 3 is 14.97 metres long, so it just makes it under the size that requires the skipper to have certification, either a French Peniche Plaisance license or an International Certificate of Competence with an Inland Endorsement. At 4.65 metres beam, it comfortably fits into the 5.1 metre locks with a bit of space left over. It is designed to maximize internal volume and it has three equal sized cabins each with convertible twin/double beds and an optional fold-down bed for child or teenager in each cabin. Each cabin has its own en-suite bathroom with shower, sink and electric-flush toilet. There is plenty of storage in these spacious hotel-style staterooms and each has air-conditioning with individual thermostats for maximum personal comfort. A fourth optional bed for one is on a convertible bunk in salon.

The design allows large windows, offering maximum interior light. There is great visibility from the salon, which shares the space with the galley. This modern kitchen has a gas oven and stove, a microwave, and a large refrigerator/freezer and it is fully equipped for preparing gourmet feasts or simple meals. Full-standing headroom of 2 meters and the level flooring throughout add to the sense of luxury accommodation.

The interior steering position is a real plus in rainy weather, and access to the foredeck from the saloon makes line handling easy. A second steering position outside on fly deck offers the skipper excellent visibility in locks and when coming alongside a mooring. Also on the upper deck are a barbecue hot plate, a bar fridge, a sink, and a cupboard for entertaining and alfresco dining in style. The boat is also equipped with a collapsible sun canopy for cruising in bright sunshine or manoeuvring in the rain.

The boats from Le Boat are equipped with all the necessary safety equipment: life ring, life jackets, boat hook, fenders and a basic first aid kit. There are comfortable beds with pillows and linen as well as bath towels and tea towels. Warm air heating and fans for cooling are included, and on some models there is air-conditioning. Also on some models with outside space, there are table, chairs and a parasol.

A Look at the Rental Boat

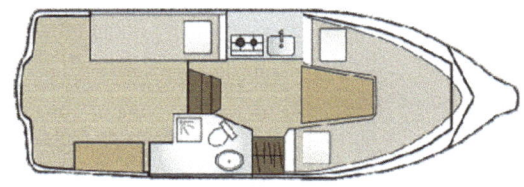

Canalous offers boats in four categories: Access, Budget, Classic and Premium in a range of sizes from one cabin to five. At the small end of the Canalous Budget category is the Fred 700, which packs a lot into its 7 metres length and 2.5 metre beam. It has a double V-berth in the fore cabin with an adjacent washroom and shower and the bench in the lounge converts to a single bed. The galley has a sink, a refrigerator and a cooktop, but no oven. Pillows and blankets are provided, but the sheets and pillowcases are not, nor are bath, hand and tea towels. All of these are available to rent at most of the bases.

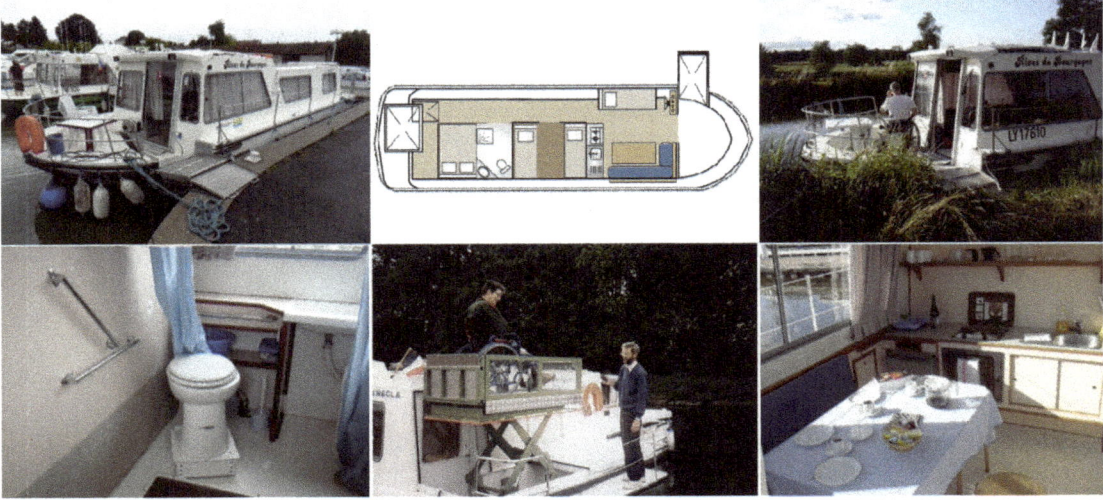

The Access models are primarily for people in wheelchairs or with other mobility problems. The Espade 1230 Handy is 12.3 metres long with a beam of 3.6 metres and has accommodation for five in two cabins, plus a convertible settee in the salon. The centre cabin has two single berths with adjustable height and anti-bedsore mattress. The rear cabin has a double berth and a single berth plus a convertible space for a child. Between the cabins is a washroom with a wheelchair accessible shower, a washbasin and swivel bracket and handrails. Supplied are sheets and pillowcases plus bath, hand and tea towels.

The entire boat is accessible by wheelchair, including the sunroof by use of electric and hydraulic lifts and there is a broad ramp for wheeled access to and from the boat. The interior is laid-out with wide doorways and corridors to allow easy manoeuvrability.

Canal Cruising in France

At the top end of the Canalous range is the Tarpon 49 Quattro Prestige. At 14.96 metres in length, it is just under the 15 metre size that requires the skipper to have the appropriate inland navigation certification. Its beam of 4.2 metres gives it less than a metre of spare width in the standard locks, but the bow thruster can ease the handling. There are two steering positions, one below in the main salon and one on the upper deck, where all-round visibility makes manoeuvring easy.

Inside, this boat boasts five cabins and a lounge with a total of twelve bed spaces. There are four double cabins with en-suite washrooms with shower, hand basin and toilet. In the salon, the settee converts to a double bed and from a separate entrance in the bow, there is a crew cabin with two single bunks and a sink. Complete bed linens are supplied, along with bath and hand towels. Interior headroom is 1.93 metres in the salon and 1.88 metres in the cabins, so head scraping should not present a problem to all but a very few. To add to the comfort, there is air-conditioning and a heating system. The boat comes with a 220V shore power connection and an inverter, which feeds the flat screen TV and the DVD player.

The galley is fully equipped for gourmet cooking, with gas cooktop, oven, refrigerator, freezer, dishwasher, coffee maker, toaster and juicer. It comes with a full inventory of table and kitchen ware: quality crockery, cutlery, glasses, pots and pans as well as table cloths and tea towels. Environmentally friendly cleaning supplies are also provided.

Up top there is wooden deck furniture, a small fridge and a deck shower with hot and cold water, extending the feeling of luxuriousness.

With the boats in the Canalous fleet, the supplied amenities vary between the levels of quality: with the basic, you need to bring your own bedding or rent it; with the premium, there is air conditioning, dishwashers, and needless to say, towels and bed linens.

A Look at the Rental Boat

Nicols builds their own boats and have been doing so for more than twenty-five years. Its range includes twenty-two models, which are a refinement from their long experience building and renting boats to suit the evolving market. Perfect for first time cruisers, the "Primo®" is the latest self-drive cruiser from the Nicols boatyard. It is a simple yet elegant model with a modern interior. For a boat slightly under 8 metres in length, the living area is very spacious and bright, thanks to its ample 3.4 metre beam, large windows and the opening glass roof, which was inspired skylights in cars.

The front cabin offers a double bed, plenty of storage space and en-suite access to the washroom with toilet, hand basin and shower. If accommodation is required for an additional person or two small children, the table and bench in the living area convert into a comfortable bed.

At the rear of the boat the outside deck is on the same level as the living area and is accessed through glass doors, which when opened extend the feeling of space and add to the views out over the water. The galley is equipped with a fridge, a freezer, a two burner cook top and an oven. Nicols' main objective for producing the "Primo®" is to provide an affordable option that will ensure that boating holidays remain accessible for every budget. To maintain this low cost objective, bathroom and kitchen towels and cloths are not included in the rental price. You can bring your own, or for a small charge, you can pick-up linen packs from the base on your arrival. The rental bathroom pack contains a hand towel, a glove towel and a larger bath towel and the kitchen linen pack has a tea towel and two dish cloths.

This is a great little boat not only for beginners, but it is also well suited for seasoned cruisers who wish to be very comfortably alone.

Canal Cruising in France

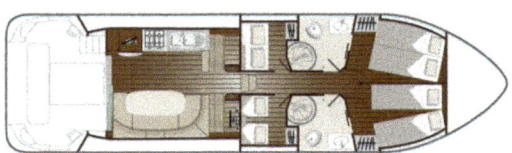

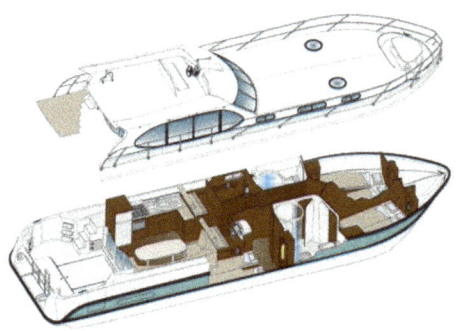

The Nicols Octo from the Estivale range is 13.5 metres long and 3.8 metres wide. It is designed with four cabins, two of which have convertible beds (either a double bed or twin beds), making this boat ideal for four couples or two couples and four children. In addition the couch in the salon converts to a double bed. The large windows all around the living area offer a 360° panoramic view that not only adds to the feeling of spaciousness, but also affords the skipper excellent visibility while using the inside steering position.

The galley is fully fitted with a large fridge and freezer, a four-burner gas cooktop and an oven. It is equipped with all the necessary pots, pans and utensils needed to prepare gourmet meals and all the crockery, cutlery and glassware to serve and enjoy them. For entertainment there is a TV, a Radio, and a CD/MP3 player and the boat is equipped with a 220 Volt shore power connection cord.

From the main salon a sliding door leads out onto the aft deck, which offers an extension to the living space and is a great place for relaxing and dining alfresco. Above it is a sliding sun awning to provide a sun shade if needed. Up top is a second steering position that offers the skipper an open pilotage position with great all-round visibility, very useful when manoeuvring into locks or alongside a mooring. An electric bow thruster makes handling much easier and adds to manoeuvring options in tight spaces. The outside spaces also include a deck shower and bathing ladder.

As with all Nicols boats, the washroom and galley linen are not included, so you either need to bring your own or rent some from the base for a small fee when you pick-up your boat.

A Look at the Rental Boat

 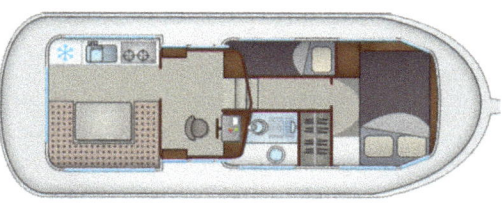

Most of the boats in the Locaboat fleet are of the "Pénichette" style. At the smaller end of these models is the 935, a 9.3 metre long boat with a beam of 3.1 metres. This compact boat has a double bed in its fore cabin and a single in the corridor, making it an ideal choice for a couple with a child. The dinette settee in the salon converts to a double bed offering accommodation for an additional couple or larger family.

The galley has a cooktop, a fridge and a sink and comes with the pots, pans and utensils necessary to prepare your meals and the crockery, cutlery and glassware to serve and enjoy them. Bed, bath and galley linens are supplied with all boats in the Locaboat fleet.

Among the interesting offerings from Locaboat is a high quality steel Dutch cruiser, the Linssen Grand Sturdy 34.9 from a company building high-end cruising yachts since 1949. This 10.7 metre long model with its 3.4 metre beam offers elegance, high-quality furnishings and comfortable cruising. Linsen's many decades of boat building experience have taught them to make optimum use of space with very functional layouts that have high quality finish and decor. This small boat provides very comfortable accommodation for four, and with the convertible salon sofa, it can house up to six.

The central living area combines the galley and the lounge, which has a sofa and table, as well as a desk/navigation corner. The sofa can be easily transformed into a large double bed, thanks to Linssen's clever 'Easy Sleep Convert' system. The forward cabin has a double bed, space for hanging clothes and a chest of drawers. Adjacent to this cabin is washroom with toilet and basin and across from it is a large separate shower. The rear cabin also contains a double bed and hanging and storage space for clothes, and it has an en-suite washroom with toilet, basin and a large shower.

Above the aft cabin is the upper deck with the helm position, which offers excellent all-round visibility. Handling the boat is made easier with thrusters in both the bow and the stern. With its traditional teal deck, this is a great place to relax and socialize either underway or alongside and it comes with a folding Bimini top.

At the upper end of the Locaboat fleet is the Pénichette 1500FB, the FB standing for Flying Bridge. It is 14.9 metres long with a beam of 3.85 metres and it incorporates four cabins, each with a double bed that is easily convertible to a pair of twins. In addition each cabin has an upper pullman berth that can expand accommodation from eight to twelve. Each cabin has a hanging cupboard and storage space and an en-suite washroom with wash basin, electric toilet and shower.

There are 230 V sockets in the main salon supplied by a shore power connection and solar panels help keep the battery charged. There is a large fully-equipped galley in which to create gourmet meals. An inside steering position in the main salon provides comfortable control, and for greater visibility and fresh air, there is a helm position on the fly bridge; both have controls for the bow thruster. Surrounding the upper helm is a table, seat bench and chairs for outside relaxing, dining and socializing. This is a comfortably roomy boat with 1.98 metre headroom throughout, except for the still generous 1.9 metres in the fore cabin.

A Look at the Rental Boat

The foregoing are just a small sampling of the range of boats offered by the four national companies and much more detail can be found on the websites of each company:

- Le Boat - www.leboat.com
- Canalous - www.canalous-plaisance.fr
- Nicols - www.boat-renting-nicols.co.uk
- Locaboat - www.locaboat.com

In choosing a boat, be aware that some boats are available in certain areas and not in others, and of course, some boat styles may be completely committed for the time you wish to rent. The websites all have grids or other pages to show model availability across bases and dates. Early booking will ensure you get the boat style you want in the area you wish to explore on the dates you choose. Also, early booking discounts are often offered.

Chapter Seven

A Look at the Locks

The type of lock that is used exclusively these days on rivers and canals is the pound lock. These have gates at each end of the chamber to control the level of water and regardless of size, they all have the same basic components and work on the same basic principle.

The hinged mitred gates open upstream and allow the force of the water to keep them closed when in use. The opening and closing mechanism varies widely The horizontal wheel,

which looks like a small table in the photo on the left is one of the variations, the pair of huge oak balance beams on the right is another. A crank, either on the top or the side of a vertical pylon is another. Many of the locks in the popular areas of France are now hydraulically operated, either through an automated cycle initiated by the boater, or by buttons pushed by a lock keeper. In the smaller locks, the sluices or paddles to allow water into and out of the lock chamber are commonly located in the gates. These are operated by a hand crank, or hydraulically in automated locks. In some locks, particularly the larger ones, there are ground sluices that

A Look at the Locks

carry the water through conduits under or beside the gates. Mooring arrangements for transiting vessels are provided in each lock. These may be as simple as bollards along the rim of the chamber, in higher locks, they could be a series of bollards in indents in the chamber walls. Sometimes there are thick vertical pipes set in recesses in the chamber walls around which to loop a line and the easiest to use are the floating bollards that rise and fall with the water level.

Regardless of the mechanisms, the basic operating principle of a lock is as follows:

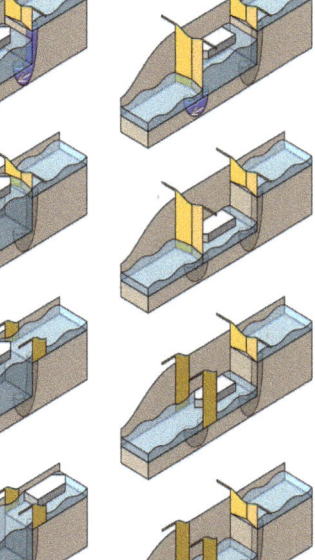
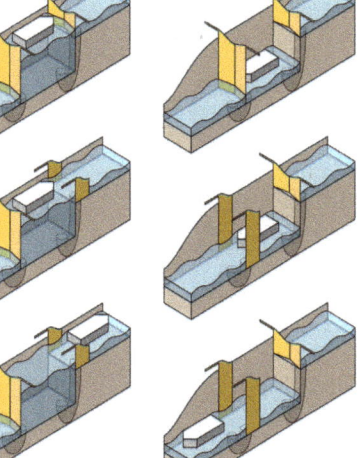

Ascending	Descending
The barge enters the lock chamber through the open downstream gates.	The barge enters the lock chamber through the open upstream gates.
The crew secure the barge in the chamber with lines to mooring points.	The crew secure the barge in the chamber with lines to mooring points.
The downstream gates are closed.	The upstream gates are closed.
The upstream sluices are opened to begin filling the chamber.	The downstream sluices are opened to begin draining the chamber.
The barge rises as the level of water fills the chamber.	The barge falls as the water drains from the chamber.
When the chamber is full, the pressure comes off the upstream gates and they can be opened.	When the chamber has emptied, the pressure comes off the downstream gates and they can be opened.
After the gates have opened the barge heads out into the upstream canal.	After the gates have opened the barge heads out into the downstream canal.

As well as there being different types of pound locks and different methods of operation, locks differ dramatically in size. At the small end of the size scale in France are the locks of Canal de l'Ourcq, which runs eastward from Paris. These are only 3.2 metres wide and offer only 0.8 metres depth. At the other extreme of the size scale is Écluse François 1er, which takes deep sea vessels into the port of Le Havre from the tidal waters of the English Channel. It is 400 metres long and 67 metres wide. In another dimension, Écluse Bollène on the Rhône River has the highest rise and fall of any lock in France at 22.5 metres. Its chamber is 190 metres long and 11.4 metres wide. However, the majority of the locks in France are the standard Freycinet gauge, built to take barges 38.5 metres long, 5.05 metres wide, 1.8 metres draft and providing a clearance of 3.5 metres under bridges.

The standard French lock has parallel, vertical-sided chamber walls. However, the locks of the Canal du Midi were designed with curved sides with a very slight slope to the walls. This design was adopted to add strength, and it seems to have worked. The original stonework from the 1670s and 80s is still mostly intact and remarkably preserved.

The entrances to the Midi locks are 5.8 metres wide, but inside the chamber the width increases to a maximum of 11 metres at the centre, allowing two 20-metre barges to lie side-by-side.

A Look at the Locks

Another type of lock chamber that is occasionally seen is the sloped wall. To make it easier and safer to use these, many have been fitted with floating pontoons that ride up and down on rails attached to the sloping wall. On the pontoons are mooring bollards, and the method of use is to simply moor the barge as one would to a float in a marina. The one pictured here is along the Yonne River between Auxerre and Migennes.

L'écluse Ronde d'Agde gives another type of lock. This one is near the Mediterranean end of the Canal du Midi, where it is necessary to cross the Hérault River. Because at this point, both the river and the canal are near sea level and at similar elevations, there was no way to provide the canal with an aqueduct over the river. To solve the problem, in 1680 a round lock was built with three sets of gates. Coming in through the set of gates to the east is up-bound canal traffic and

river traffic from upstream of the weir. Once the gates close, the traffic can choose either to be lowered into the downstream portion of the river and head out the gates to the south toward the Mediterranean, or to be lifted to the continuation of the canal and exit through the gates to the west. This was a very elegant seventeenth century solution to the problem and it continues to serve well to this day.

Regardless the shapes of the locks, it is necessary to stabilize the barge in the chamber while the water level is being changed, and this is particularly important in the up-bound direction. The turbulence of the incoming water wants to move the barge around, sometimes rather violently and this movement needs to controlled.

To assist in the control of the vessel during the ascent or descent, locks are fitted with a wide variety of devices. Mostly, these are fixed bollards along the lip of the chamber. In some locks these are plentiful, well-spaced and in good condition. In other locks, there are missing bollards, almost always exactly where they are most needed, thus requiring the juggling of the barge into position to use what exists and even then having to resort to creative line-handling.

When heading upstream through higher locks, it is often nearly impossible to toss a line over the bollards from the deck of the barge, let alone see the bollards from below. This requires the crew to disembark before the lock and walk up to receive the tossed lines as the barge enters.

When there is no easy place to disembark, the chamber ladder is used to access the rim of the lock. The ladder is dirty and slimy, since it is regularly in and out of the water as the lock fills and empties. In this photo we can see from the line of slime on the wall that the fill level of the chamber is nearly two metres below the rim. This added to the three metre rise of the lock makes the likelihood of ringing an unseen bollard with a line toss from the deck of the barge extremely remote.

To complicate the situation even further, often with locks near populated centres or in areas of high tourism, there have been safety barriers placed around the chambers. Most often these interfere with the easy and safe use of the locks by boaters. This photo shows how a safety barrier on the Canal du Centre makes it nearly impossible to use the only upstream bollards in the lock. The placement of the barrier precludes throwing a bight of line up from the deck to ring the bollard. To use it requires the crew to climb the ladder to the lip of the chamber and then to move into a very awkward and dangerous position to place a line over the bollard. We continue to tell the lock keepers that these safety barriers are dangerous for boaters. It seems that theoretical engineers with no canal boating experience are responsible.

In some of the higher locks, in-chamber arrangements are provided for mooring. Among these is the vertical series of mooring points in recesses up the wall. These are generally spaced about a metre and a half apart, so two are always within reach. It is easier and safer to use two lines, placing the next one before removing the existing one. With this type of mooring point, it is possible for the lines to become jammed both when ascending and descending.

As with all line handling in a lock chamber, it is dangerous to tie or cleat a line, even temporarily. It can be easily forgotten and quickly become a potentially deadly weapon as the barge tightens against it to an explosive breaking. Even if the line doesn't break, a jammed, cleated or tied line can rip out or damage the boat's mooring bitts or cleats. The boat can hang-up in the lock and require the filling or draining cycle to be stopped and reversed.

Another type of in-chamber mooring is the vertical pipe. With these, the mooring line, or a bight of it is passed around the pipe and held. As the barge moves up or down in the chamber, the line slides along the pipe. Care must be taken to closely monitor the lines, ensuring they continue to move up or down with the barge. We have found many of these arrangements with heavily corroded pipes that offer great resistance to the free sliding of the line. Even the coating of slime on the pipes does little to overcome this friction. The lines need to be jiggled, flipped and jostled frequently through the process to prevent binding.

Also, it is essential that the integrity of the system be tested before committing the load of the barge to it. It may not be securely attached to the lock. We have seen several with loose anchors on the lock rims. One on Canal de Garonne nearly collapsed on us. There are also many with their pipes missing, making them useless.

A Look at the Locks

Along the series of locks leading down from the aqueduct across the Garonne River at Agen, the lock infrastructure is in deplorable condition. Most of the pipes are missing from the vertical slots, safety fencing makes it very difficult to access the few bollards on the chamber rim, and deep fissures and cracks in the masonry of the chamber lip make jamming a mooring line a distinct possibility. Creative mooring and very close attention to the lines is necessary throughout the entire locking process.

In some locks the lack of suitable bollards or the unsuitable placement of them, makes motoring against a spring the only viable mooring arrangement. This entails leading a line forward from the bow or stern, or from both and then engaging the engine astern to pull against the lines while using the helm to keep the barge against the chamber wall. This can also be done by motoring forward against lines led aft.

In some locks with difficult access to the chamber rim, fixed lines are suspended down the sides of the chamber to be used for securing the barge. In this photo taken in the lock below the town of Clairac on the Lot River, we used the suspended lines, but their placement put our rudder in the way of the downstream gates when they closed. There was no convenient alternative but to motor forward against the line while keeping a very close watch on the line dangling down the opposite wall, lest its submerged end be pulled into our turning propeller.

Not all lock mooring arrangements are as cantankerous as these, many of the very large locks have floating bol-

lards set in vertical bays in the chamber walls. Most often these are spaced at intervals of 30 metres or more, making securing to one at the bow and one at the stern very difficult and impracticable for most pleasure boats, which are generally much shorter than this. The easiest way for a vessel shorter than about 25 metres is to stop the barge centred on the bollard and take the bow and stern lines to the bollard. Always ensure that the bollard is free to move in its slot before committing to it. This can be done by carefully adding some body weight to it with a foot. Closely monitor the movement of the float throughout the locking process, being prepared to quickly adjust the lines or remove them if the float jams in its ways.

Besides the mooring arrangements, variation among locks is also found with the gate designs and their opening mechanisms. Gates are the watertight doors which seal the lock chamber from the upper and lower pounds. On most smaller locks, the gates are a pair of mitred doors hinged to the sides at each end of the chamber. Most commonly the doors are mitred so that when closed, the pair meets at a broad angle like a chevron pointing upstream. The pressure from only a slight difference in water-level will squeeze the closed gates tightly together. This reduces the leaks between the doors and prevents their being opened until water levels have equalised. Here on a Canal du Nivernais lock, the gates have just been swung closed with the balance beams, the weight of which balance the non-floating portion of the oak gates to take pressure off their hinges.

In this photo of slightly more modern lock gate system on the Canal du Nivernais, the water in the pound has just arrived at the level of the upstream pound, releasing the pressure against the gates and allowing them to be cranked open. Here the opening mechanism is a pair of columns each with a hand crank that drives bevel gears that turn a shaft with a pinion on its lower end that moves a rack that is attached to its gate.

A Look at the Locks

The downstream gates of a lock need to be taller than the upstream gates since they have to seal off the full chamber, whereas the upper gates need only hold back the upper pound. The lower gate's height is the sum of the lift of the lock and the depth of water downstream of it. In some locks the lift is so high that a full height gate is impracticable. Here is an example from the Canal de Roanne à Digoin in which a solid end wall closes the portion above the downstream gates. The chamber fills to just below the top of the wall.

In this lock the doors are opened and closed using a pair of hand cranks on columns set on the end wall. Because of the weight of the doors the shaft and bevel gear system is run through reducing gears to give greater mechanical advantage, making the cranking process very long.

Another type of gate found on the deeper locks is one that lifts to allow the traffic to pass under it. Pictured below is Écluse Bollène on the Rhône. At its upstream end, the gate sinks beneath the water, allowing the traffic to pass over the top of it.

The gates of the larger locks are electrically or hydraulically operated. It would be nearly impossible to move such massive gates by hand. During the past two decades, many of the locks on the Freycinet gauge canals have also been automated. On many of these canals, it is the boater that operates the locks. This is done with a variety of systems, ranging from remote control units to lock-side control panels.

The photo on the left, above shows the hand-held remote control box that is issued on the Canal entre Champagne et Bourgogne. The photo beside it shows one of the new user-operated automatic control pylons installed at lock side near the summit of the Canal du Midi. While the locks along the Canal du Midi have all been automated, all except a very few are still operated by lock keepers.

This photo shows one of the earlier forms of remote control that still exist on many of the French canals. A dangling rod is suspended above the canal a few hundred metres before the lock. Giving it a proper twist sets the lock cycle in motion and usually gets a response from the traffic lights at the lock. Depending on the canal, the response can be a flashing orange light and/or the light changing from red to red and green, indicating that the lock is being prepared, or to green indicating that the lock is ready to be entered. Sometimes there is no response from the lights and the boater is left guessing whether the signal was received, whether the lights are malfunctioning or whether the entire system is malfunctioning. The solution is to wait a while, then moor and walk up to the lock for a look. There are call boxes in the lock that connect directly to VNF.

Chapter Eight

Basic Boat Handling

During my training in the Royal Canadian Navy in the 1960s and 70s, as I learned the theory and skills necessary for the safe command and control of Her Majesty's ships, many fundamental thoughts were impressed on me. These served me very well in my naval career and they have continued to serve with my pleasure boating ever since. The following are some of the thoughts that pertain to handling a ship near land:

- Land is a navigational hazard to be avoided;
- Never approach land faster than you are willing to hit it;
- Moving slowly is moving safely;
- Ships handle somewhat like cars with bald tires on slick ice;
- Ships maintain their current direction unless propelled in a new direction;
- The rudder moves the stern of the ship, not the bow;
- The rudder has no effect unless there is water movement past it;
- When meeting another ship never assume its skipper knows what he is doing;
- When in doubt, stop the ship;
- Ships have no brakes;
- Where you see birds wading, assume the water is shallow;

These are all common sense ideas, some very simplistic, but taken together, remembered and adhered to, they will keep you safe and make your boat-handling much easier.

The first three can be considered together. The vast majority of shipping accidents involve land, either by running into pieces of it above or below water, or by colliding with other shipping while trying to avoid hitting land. A safe speed for a ship near land is one which will allow it to stop before hitting something or at least enable it to slow to a speed where minimal damage will result. For boats on canals and rivers, land is always nearby, so the risk of running aground or of hitting the bank is constant. Moving slowly is the rule, and fortunately in the French canals there are speed limits to reduce the erosion of the canal banks from boat wakes. The canal speed limits are usually 8 kilometres per hour or slower.

The next four fundamental thoughts deal with controlling the movement of ships and we'll consider them together. Just as a car on slick ice will continue along in the same direction when the steering wheel is turned, a ship or boat will drift in the direction it had been going even though the helm has turned the rudder to toward a new direction. On a flat-bottomed barge this side slip will be more severe than it is on a boat with a deep V-shaped hull or a keel.

Even when the bow is pointing in the new direction, the vessel will drift sideways, wanting to continue in the direction it had been going. In order for it to move in the new direction, power must be applied during the turn and especially when the bow is pointing in the new direction. With this in mind, the best way to handle a tight turn is to slow before it and then slowly accelerate as the helm is applied, powering the boat as it swings to the new heading. This will dramatically reduce side slip and move the boat cleanly around the bend.

While manoeuvring in tight quarters, always be aware that it is the stern of the vessel that moves when the helm is turned. If the helm is turned to starboard, the stern swings to port as the vessel pivots on its vertical axis, which is a long way forward. The sharper the turn, the more the swing, so always ensure you have sufficient room and water depth opposite the turn for the stern to swing.

One of the most common mistakes among beginning boaters is thinking that when the helm is turned the boat will turn in a fashion similar to steering a car. The car's tires grip the road, but the boat's hull does not grip the water. With a boat, response to the helm is slow so the helmsman must avoid the mistake of over-steering The process should be: turn the helm, wait for a response, wait to see the effect, adjust as necessary. Remember, slowly is safely.

The more water flow there is past the rudder, the quicker the response, but with no water flow past the rudder it offers no control. The wash from the propeller turning forward gives sufficient flow over the rudder to make it effective even at low speed, so if a turn is needed at a very slow speed, applying a little power will assist. With the propeller turning astern its wash is directed forward and away from the rudder, giving a considerable reduction in the water flow past the rudder. For this reason, there is little directional control when a boat begins to move astern. Helm control increases as the boat picks-up sternway.

When meeting another ship never assume that its skipper knows what he is doing or that he will do the standard, correct and predictable things when manoeuvring around you. This is particularly true on the canals near rental boat bases and even more so if it is at the beginning of a rental cycle, when there will be many neophyte skippers desperately trying to learn how to handle their very first boat. Don't assume either that a private boat or a commercial barge will always manoeuvre in the standard, correct and predictable manner, though most often they will. Always be prepared to take avoiding action or to stop.

When in doubt, stop the ship, but understand that except for the anchor, there are no brakes aboard. Since dropping the anchor to stop in an emergency will almost invariably take more time and space than is available, this is not a viable option. A better option is to always be prepared, to always have in mind a series of 'What ifs?' and to always have multiple answers for each of them. As you approach a blind bend in a narrow canal, ask yourself:

- "What if a large commercial barge is approaching from just out of sight?"
- "What if a speeding rental boat is zigzagging toward the bend?"
- "What if there are two boats untangling from a collision in the bend?"
- "What if there is a boat coming around the bend on the wrong side of the canal?"
- "What if there is a large tree branch or entire tree freshly fallen into the canal?"
- "What if there is a group of kayaks spread-out around the bend?"

The safe skipper will navigate with thoughts like these in mind and will always be ready to respond appropriately. The easiest answer to all of these when approaching a sharp blind bend is to approach slowly. Besides, approaching slowly has the additional benefit of allowing you to accelerate around the turn and substantially reduce side slip.

Prop Walk

When stopping the boat, another force comes into play. The turn of the propeller has a paddle wheel effect commonly called 'prop walk', which moves the stern sideways. Propellers are made either right-hand or left-hand, which is to say that the angles of the blades are set one way or the other. With a right-hand propeller, the boat moves forward when the propeller turns to the right or clockwise when viewed from the stern. Starting forward with a right-hand propeller, the stern swings to starboard. Going astern, the prop walk takes the stern to port. Prop walk is the result of a combination of forces caused by the lower blades being in denser water than the upper blades, the bottom effect from the shallow water and the downward angle of the propeller shaft, among others.

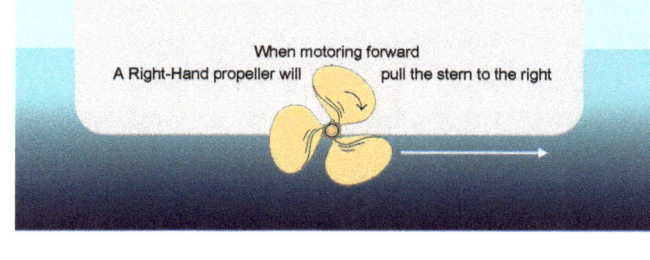

So, in stopping a boat, as a right-hand propeller begins to turn astern, the prop walk begins to slowly move the stern to the left. As the boat slows in speed, the prop walk movement increases, and unless it is countered, the boat will end-up cross-wise in the canal. To counter the effect when stopping, turn the helm to port, adjusting the rudder angle to keep the boat straight as it slows to a stop. If the helm angle is insufficient to stop the swing, shift to neutral, pause and then give a short burst in forward gear. The propwash on the rudder will quickly deflect the stern back to where you want it, and you can shift back to astern gear to continue the stop.

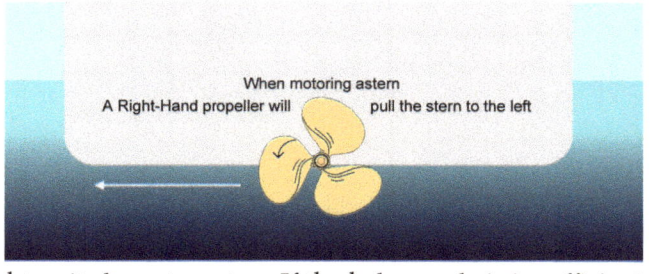

Prop walk can be used to advantage in boat handling. Knowing the amount of the effect on a particular boat can ease many common boat-handling manoeuvres. Coming alongside in a lock chamber or to a mooring on a wharf or a float, a left-hand propeller prefers the starboard side. In leaving a lock chamber or a mooring alongside to starboard, a left-hand propeller allows you to simply motor ahead, the prop walk will move the stern away from the chamber wall, wharf or bank and you can add a touch of port helm to move the bow off as the boat gains speed and the stern gains swing room. With a right-hand propeller, moorings on the port side are preferred and all the actions and movements are reversed from those outlined above, and they are just as easy.

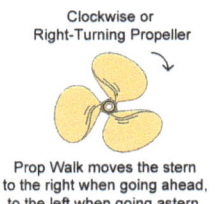
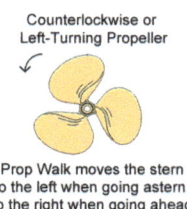

Another way to use prop walk to advantage is in turning around in a narrow space. A boat will turn more sharply in the direction opposite to the prop walk. A right-hand propeller rotating clockwise to move the boat forward will have a prop walk component that wants to move the stern to the right. To turn about sharply, stop or nearly stop away from the bank, leaving sufficient room for the stern to swing to starboard. Put the helm hard over to port and give a burst in forward gear, then haul back to slow ahead. The stern will swing to the right from the rudder and this swing will be accentuated by the prop walk. The boat will pivot around its vertical axis for a considerable time before it picks-up much forward way. A short burst of higher engine speed from time to time will quicken the rotation.

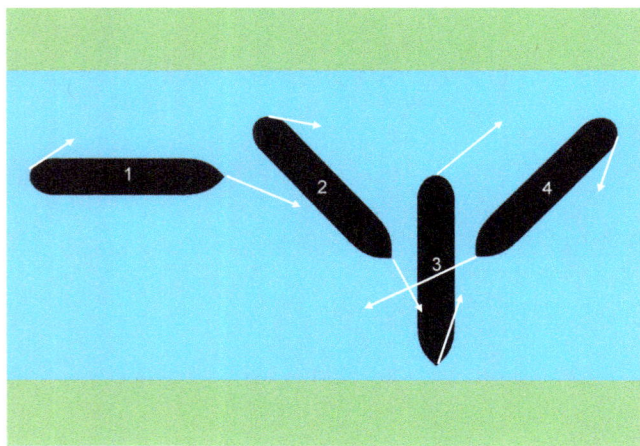

In a canal that is too narrow to make it around in one turn, and some back and forth jogs are required, it is preferable to turn in the opposite direction. Again we will consider this with the right-hand propeller, which is the more common. Stop or nearly stop away from the bank, leaving sufficient room for the stern to swing to port. (1) Put the helm hard over to starboard and give a burst in forward gear, then haul back to slow ahead. (2) The stern will swing to the left from the rudder and the swing will be accentuated by the prop walk. The boat will pivot around its vertical axis for a considerable time before it picks-up much forward way. (3) As the bow nears the bank, shift into astern gear and increase the engine speed to stop the boat. The boat will continue to spin clockwise, now augmented by the prop walk pulling the stern to port. (4) As the stern approaches the bank, shift into forward gear and give the engine a burst to stop the stern way and to add a large water flow over the rudder, which is still hard to starboard and will accelerate the pivot of the boat. With practice, one jog or at most two should allow a barge to turn about in very little more width than its length.

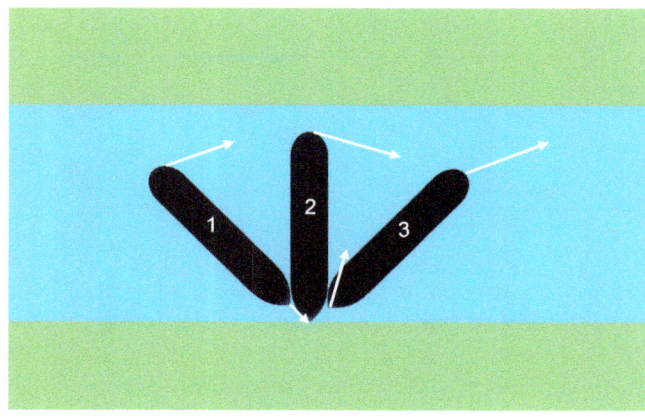

Sometimes the canal is too narrow to conveniently do the back and fill, so another method is used. (1) Following the first two steps above, turn to gently place the bow of the boat against the bank. Keeping the rudder hard over, (2) use the engine in slow ahead to wash water over the rudder and add to the prop walk effect to swing the stern around sufficiently (3) to back off a bit and continue the turn. This illustration is for a left-hand propeller; you would use the other bank for a right-hand one.

You can also use prop walk to advantage when mooring. Here we will look at my favourite propeller turn, the left-hand. It is ideal for coming alongside starboard-side-to in very tight quarters. Slowly approach the desired gap along the quai at a shallow angle As the stern passes the bow of the ship astern, shift into astern

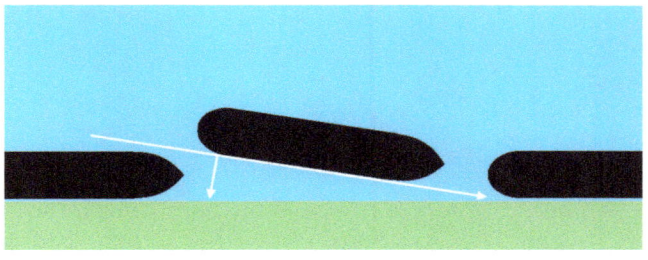

gear and allow the prop walk to carry your stern in as your vessel slows to a stop. This will bring you very close alongside and parallel to the face of the quai and all that is required is to drop your mooring lines over the bollards. This trick works equally well with a right-hand screw when mooring on the opposite bank.

Using prop walk as an assistant rather than as a problem is one of the keys to proper boat handling. Knowing its effects and using them to your advantage makes for smooth, efficient and professional-looking manoeuvres and they become second nature as experience builds with a boat or a barge. The major secret to success is in doing everything slowly and watching the response. Winds and currents, if there are any, will affect the process, but a sense of its overall evolution will develop with experience, and appropriate compensation for external forces will become natural. In many ways it is like dancing with a partner whose moves and responses you understand and with whom you move in harmony. Gracefully and effortlessly dancing with a boat on a canal is a joy.

Entering and Leaving Locks

The most common canal locks in France are built to the Freycinet gauge, devised in 1878 to standardize the canals. The chambers are designed to accommodate a standard péniche, which is 5.05 metres wide and 38.5 metres long. For a century and a half, péniche skippers have been threading into lock chambers that are only a few centimetres wider and longer than their barges. The secret is to line-up in advance and move slowly, allowing the momentum to carry the barge into the chamber. This works well also for smaller barges and boats. However; there are sometimes external forces, such as cross-winds or the current from a bypass sluice that dumps water across the canal below the downstream gates. The lighter the boat, the more affected it will be by these.

To compensate for a crosswind there are two easy procedures. The first is to set-up the boat on the upwind side of the centreline and allow the wind to push the boat back toward the centreline as it approaches the lock entrance. The second is to set-up on the centreline and crab along it into

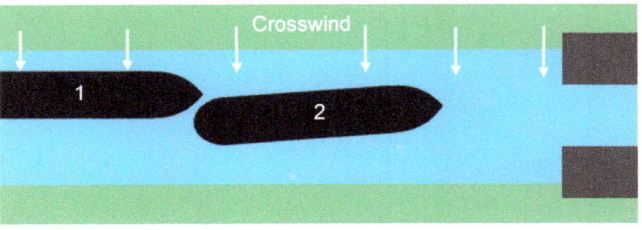

the wind. Both of these require seat-of-the-pants manoeuvring, adjusting and compensating as conditions change on the approach. In high winds, a faster approach will offer better control, but the consequences of a misjudgement are more severe. These procedures work equally well when approaching narrow bridge holes, which are often the same width as the locks.

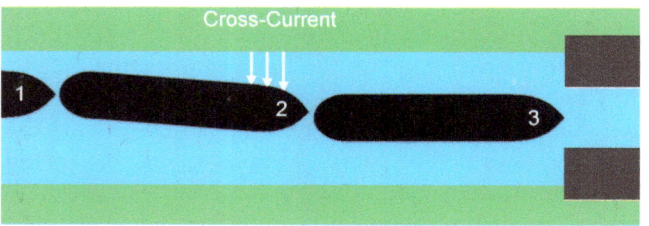

One of the other approach problems is the cross-current from the discharge of excess water from upstream. This current can vary from non-existent to very strong. The method of manoeuvring through the side current is the same for all strengths. (1) Once the lock is ready to be entered, set-up offset from the centreline toward the side with the source of the current. (2) As the bow passes through the current, it will be pushed off line. Do not try to stop or correct this swing; it will soon stop. As the centre of the boat passes the current, the boat will be pushed sideways, still at an angle to the centreline. Do not try to compensate for this. (3) As the stern of the boat reaches the current, it will be swung, realigning the boat with the centreline. If your assessment of the amount of offset was correct, you will exit the cross-current on the centreline and aligned with the entrance. Pat yourself on the back. If not, some adjustments will be needed. Again, with much of boat handling, experience and practice make it progressively easier.

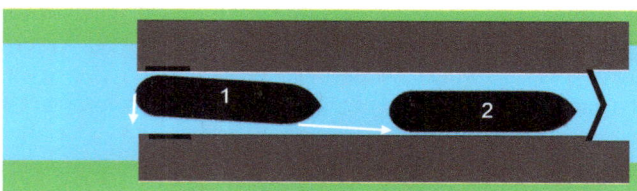

If possible, always secure in a lock chamber on your boat's preferred side, which with a left-hand propeller is the starboard side and with a right-hand propeller, the port side. Enter the lock slightly offset toward the side away from your preferred wall, then part way into the chamber, (1) angle the bow toward your wall and put the propeller astern. The prop walk will move the stern toward the wall as you slow to a stop and you will end up (2) with the boat straight along the wall, making it easy to pass lines to the bollards. On leaving the lock, the prop walk will move the stern away from the wall as you apply forward power. As soon as there is some swing room for the stern, begin applying a bit of helm to steer the bow off the wall. Within a few metres the boat be clear of the wall and you will have sufficient steerage to cleanly exit without bouncing and scraping.

Mooring

Mooring is the term commonly used to denote securing a boat alongside. This can be in a lock chamber or on a wharf, a jetty, a float or a canal or river bank. When selecting a mooring consider one on your favoured side so that you can use your prop walk to advantage both in arriving and departing. Not only will this make your manoeuvring easier and less stressful, but it has the added advantage of not providing entertainment to the boaters moored nearby.

Basic Boat Handling

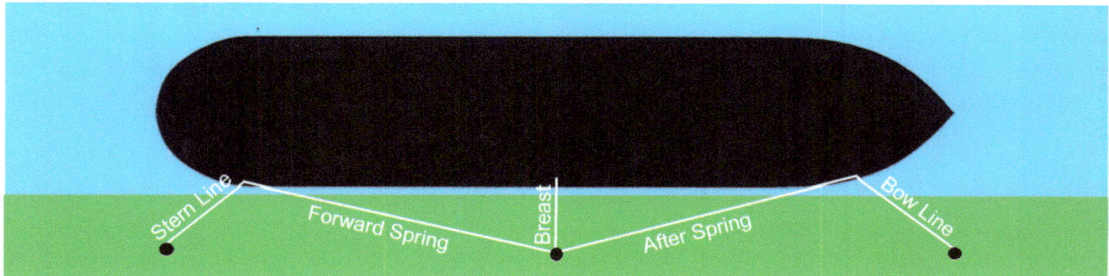

A boat is normally secured in place using mooring lines led from the boat to bollards, cleats, posts or pins ashore. Each of the mooring lines has a name, which are easy to remember because they describe their position or purpose. We'll look at the five most common ones here. The stern line generally runs out at about a 45° angle from near the stern of the boat. Its purpose is to hold the stern in and to limit the boat's movement forward. Similarly, the bow line runs out at about 45° to hold the bow to the bank and limit movement aft. The springs add in reducing a fore and aft movement of the boat. They are longer than the bow and stern lines, generally one-third to two-thirds the boat length and they are set at shallower angles. The stretch of these longer lines absorbs the energy from the suction, surge and wakes of passing canal traffic. The naming of the springs is initially counter intuitive; however, knowing that they are named for their direction of lead rather than for their location, makes sense of their names.

One of the most useful lines in coming to a mooring is the breast, but it is often ignored. It leads perpendicularly from amidships and for simplicity in mooring, it should often be the first line ashore. This single line will hold the entire side of the boat close and parallel to the mooring place, keeping both bow and stern from swinging out. With the breast snubbed to a bollard the boat is stabilized, giving the opportunity to relax and carefully set the bow, stern and spring lines.

The lines must be securely fastened to solid mooring bollards, cleats, posts or other mooring fixtures ashore to hold the boat against the forces generated by passing traffic. These are strong, much stronger than an inexperienced boater would expect. Speed limits of 3 or 4 kilometres per hour are generally imposed in haltes nautiques, ports de plaisances and other organized mooring places along the French inland waterways. These are indicated by the standard Code Européen des Voies Navigables Interieur (CEVNI) signage, like the 4 kilometres per hour speed limit sign shown here.

As a barge approaches, its hungry propeller draws down the level of water in the canal ahead of it and sucks water away from the banks. Boats moored along the banks will be pulled toward the approaching barge and then out toward the centre of the canal. As the barge passes, there will be a surge of water refilling the drained area and then the pull out and along the path of the passing barge. There will also be the suction and turbulence from its propeller as its stern passes. These multi-directional forces are considerably reduced at lower speeds, but they are still significant at 4 kilometres per hour. To counter them, even in their weakened state, you must properly secure your boat.

If you are moored along the bank in a stretch of wilderness where some inconsiderate traffic will pass you at the 8 kilometre per hour speed limit, it is essential to be well secured with long springs and well-angled bow and stern lines attached to solid mooring points. If you are mooring to pins pounded into the bank, ensure they are well angled and deeply sunk in firm ground. They will need to sustain many hundreds of kilograms of force. Considerate traffic, which will include most commercial and pleasure barges, will slow for moored boats, but do not expect rental boaters to understand.

Meeting Other Small Boats

In navigation, the term meeting refers two or more vessels each approaching the other. On the canals it is a regular event to meet other vessels that are going in opposite directions. If the channel is restricted in width, then the down-bound vessel is privileged and the up-bound vessel must give way if there is insufficient room. Generally, though there is ample room for two boats to meet without either having to slow or stop.

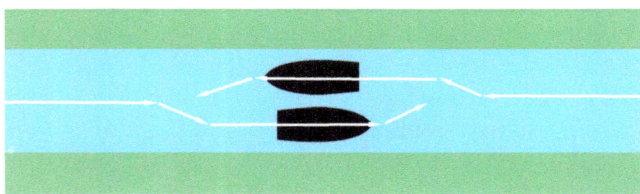

Experienced boaters will motor in the centre of the canal where the water is deeper and steerage is unaffected by the bank effect. This path is easier on fuel consumption and is less damaging to the banks. As an opposing boat approaches the experienced skipper will slow slightly and when it draws to within four or five boat lengths, he will gently turn toward the right bank, leaving more than half of the channel to the other boat. As soon as they are clear, he'll head back to the centre and move back to cruising speed. If you see this happening, don't think that the boat is playing chicken with you. Learn to do it yourself; it is safer and less damaging to the environment.

Meeting Barges

Occasionally on the small canals you will meet large barges. These could be either commercial, such as a freight or a hotel barge, or they might more commonly be private cruising barges. Whichever, they need to be met carefully. They push a large volume of water ahead as a bow wake, there is the suction along their sides from the pull of their propeller, which also causes a draw-down of the water level in the canal, there is the push of the stern wake and there is the churning and turbulent water from their propeller as you pass the stern. Knowing these forces, their sequence and their direction allows you to predict the movement of your boat and respond accordingly.

Make an approach similar to the one in the illustration and explanation above. The barge will most likely be doing the same thing and you can dance past each other with ease. Remember that the slower you go, the less control you have of your boat and the more affected it will be by the forces, so it is not a good idea to slow-down too much. Do not be tempted to correct to port as the bow wave moves you toward the bank; the suck back to port by the draw of the barge's propeller will soon correct it for you. Fine tune with the helm as necessary as you eyeball your way down the centre of the channel that remains between the barge and the bank, being ready at all times to counter the forces wanting to move you off that line.

Alternatively, if the bank is not foul and you have room and time, you can pull over to the bank and stop. Beware, though that unless you can properly moor, you will risk damage to the boat.

Chapter Nine

Line Handling and Safety in Locks

First, let's look at some basic rules and etiquette with locks. Commercial traffic has priority in the locks, so if while you are waiting for a lock to be prepared for you, a commercial barge arrives, you must let it pass to use the lock ahead of you. Even if there is room in the lock chamber for you to fit in astern of the barge, the barge skipper is allowed to deny your entry if he thinks it will cause delay. At times the lock keeper will have you wait after the lock has been prepared, even when there is no apparent reason. After a few minutes, the reason for the wait will become apparent as a barge approaches around the bend. It has priority and the lock keeper will keep its way clear so that it is not delayed. Remember, the commercial barge is working to make a living; you are cruising for pleasure.

If there is a line-up waiting for a lock, do not butt-in; take your place in the queue. Just like automobile road-rage, boat-rage can become very ugly. Remember you are cruising for pleasure, so relax and enjoy the surroundings. Besides, as you wait for your turn you can watch the boats ahead of you cycling through the lock. You can gain some ideas of methods that might make your own passage through the lock easier. If there are rental boats ahead, you will likely also see things to avoid doing.

Most accidents in canal boating occur in the locks. Some basic accident prevention practices are:

- Do not attempt to stop the movement of the boat with your hands or feet;
- Never allow any of your body parts to come between the boat and the lock wall;
- Do not try to jump the gap between the boat and the lock rim;
- Never step inside a coil of rope;
- Do not secure the mooring lines when in a descending lock, allow them to run freely;
- Do not take a full turn around a bollard when in a descending lock;
- Do not allow your attention to be distracted from the job at hand.

Many of these are self explanatory, but because they are so important to your safety, I will dwell on the reasons for each and the possible consequences of ignoring them.

Do not attempt to stop the movement of the boat with your hands or feet. The weight of the boat and its motion, even when very slow, combine to give large inertia that can easily strain muscles and often place you in risk of more serious injury. Let the fenders and bumper pads do the job for you. They are there to absorb the energy, your hands and feet are not.

Never allow any of your body parts to come between the boat and the lock wall. The weight and inertia of the boat can very easily make you an amputee. This short but graphic explanation should get the message across.

Do not try to jump the gap from the boat to the lock rim. The boat is not a stable platform from which to launch a jump. A component of your leap force will push the boat down and away, causing you to jump short and end-up in the water. If the boat is still moving, you risk being crushed between it and the lock wall or possibly having the propeller bloody the water.

Never step inside a coil of rope. A coil of mooring line can very easily and quickly tighten around a misplaced foot and trap it in a wrap that is impossible to quickly untangle. If the line continues to run out, it could pull the foot to a bollard, cleat or fairlead. Hopefully the rope tangle will serve as a tourniquet on the severe injury or the stump. Again graphic, but the point needs to be driven home.

Do not secure the mooring lines when in a descending lock, allow them to run freely. Securing a line temporarily in order to tend to something else, is the main cause of boats being hung-up in locks. Once tension comes on the line, it becomes very difficult, often impossible to undo the secured line. The boat will then hang on the line, it could possibly spill its occupants into the water, it could capsize or it could begin flooding with water. The line may snap or the mooring bollard or cleat may be ripped out of the boat, causing an extremely dangerous whip of lines, with or without hardware flailing on one end. Always allow the lines to run freely.

Do not take a full turn around a bollard when in a descending lock. As the boat descends in a lock, the mooring lines must be constantly tended to ensure they run-out freely. If you take more than a 180° turn around a bollard, you run the strong risk of developing a riding turn, which acts like a knot and stops the free run of the line. The boat will hang-up as in the previous instance with similar consequences.

Do not allow your attention to be distracted from the job at hand. During the entire locking procedure, from arrival in the chamber all the way through exiting, attention must be focused on safety. The skipper must oversee and direct all crew and not be distracted from this. Crew that have no tasks to perform should remain out of the way and refrain from any action or conversation that could distract others from their roles.

Line Handling and Safety in Locks

Now that the safety lecture is over, and with the points firmly in mind, we can relax a bit and get on with the process of locking through. The process is safe and easy as long as the correct procedures are followed.

With up-bound locks, the chamber is empty when you enter it, making the walls stand well above the deck level of the boat. It is mandatory to moor the boat in the chamber and there are many ways to do this:

- If the lock wall is low, you can toss bights of the mooring lines around the bollards;
- You can use a boat hook to reach the lines up to the bollards;
- In some locks, the lock keeper will take your lines;
- Before entering the lock you can land a crew member to walk up and receive the lines;

Regardless of the method of passing the mooring lines, they must be passed and constantly tended as the boat rises in the chamber.

Once the mooring lines have been passed, the crew can close the downstream gates or assist the lock keeper with this if the lock is manual and manned. In unmanned automatic locks, the button to continue the cycle should not be pushed until the boat has been stabilized and everyone is ready to continue. In a manned lock, the lock keeper looks for an acknowledgement that it is safe to begin filling the lock.

The water flows into the chamber through vanes or sluices in the upstream gates and sometimes through underground sluices. In some locks there is very little turbulence as the chamber fills; in others there is a great churning of water with eddies and back-eddies that move the boat around. The task of the mooring line handlers is to limit the movement of the boat to prevent damage to itself, to other boats in the chamber and possibly to the lock gates.

When the chamber has filled, leave the mooring lines on the bollards while the upstream gates open. If the lock in manually operated, have the crew open or assist the lock keeper in opening the gates. Keep the mooring lines on while other boats leave the chamber ahead of you and do not remove them until the turbulence and propeller surge and suction of the other boats has subsided.

In down-bound locks, the lines are much easer to place over the mooring bollards because they are below the deck level of your boat. The same applies to closing the upstream gates and signalling readiness to continue, as it does with the downstream ones. There is very little turbulence as the lock drains and there is little boat movement except in the downward direction. However, it is crucial that very close attention be paid to the mooring lines and that they are never secured, but always allowed to run freely as the boat descends to prevent hanging-up the boat.

When the chamber has drained, leave the mooring lines on the bollards while the downstream gates open. Again, if the lock in manually operated, have the crew open or assist the lock keeper in opening the gates. Keep the mooring lines on while other boats leave the chamber ahead of you and do not remove them until the turbulence and propeller surge and suction of the other boats has subsided.

This is a very short chapter that is very full of critical safety information. Read the chapter again to reinforce the points. Thoroughly brief your crew before you enter your first lock and ensure that they know and understand the reasons behind all the safety points and locking procedures.

Chapter Ten

Rules of the Road and CEVNI

The International Regulations for Preventing Collisions at Sea 1972, referred to as COLREGs, are published by the International Maritime Organization and they set out, among other things, the 'Rules of the Road' or navigation rules to be followed by ships and other vessels at sea to prevent collisions. The COLREGs also refer to the specific political line that divides the high seas from coastal waterways and those from inland waterways, which are each subject to their own navigation rules. The International Maritime Organization specify that these other rules should be as closely in line with the international rules as possible. In most of continental Europe, the Code Européen des Voies de la Navigation Intérieure (CEVNI) apply. The name of these regulations in English is: European Code for Navigation on Inland Waters.

Rental boaters on the French canals do not need to know all of the CEVNI manoeuvring regulations, but at a minimum they need to know the rules on meeting other vessels. Generalized and simplified, these are:

- The down-bound vessel has priority and the up-bound vessel must give way to it;
- Down-bound is defined as the direction of the water flow in a river or canal;
- When meeting other boats, steer to the right-hand side of the canal;
- A boat entering a major waterway from a minor one must give way;

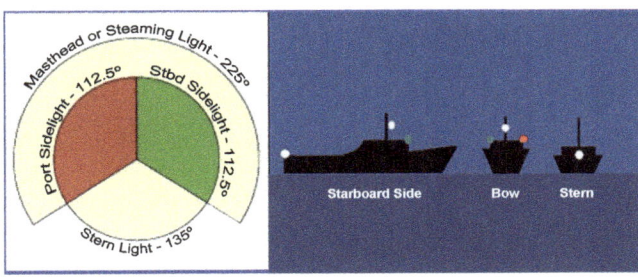

In addition to the manoeuvring rules, there regulations on navigation lights that identify the various types, purposes and activities of watercraft. Other than the standard red, green and white running lights, few of the other variations will be seen on the small waterways used by the rental boaters. Besides, since these small canals are closed to navigation at night there is no regular need to know or to use the lights. However, when visibility is obscured by rain, mist or fog, the regulations stipulate that navigation lights be used.

There are over one hundred waterways signs and markings in Annex 7 to the CEVNI regulations. Thankfully for the casual rental boater in France, not all of these will be found on the small canals. On the following page are four dozen of the more common signs.

Canal Cruising in France

Indication signals

 E1 passage allowed
 E2 Electric cable crossing
 E4 Ferry crossing with cable
 E5 Stopping allowed
 E6 Anchoring allowed
 E7 Mooring allowed

 E8 Turning point indicated
 E13 Drinking water
 E14 Phone box for boat-users
 E15 Water-skiing course

 E9a E9b  E9c
Main waterway / secondary waterway

 E10a  E10b
This waterway is classed as a tributary of the waterway you are approaching

 E11
End of restriction or obligation

Prohibition signals

 A1 Navigation forbidden
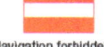 A1 Passage forbidden except for small engineless crafts
 A2 Passing and crossing forbidden
 A3 Does not affect pleasure
 A4 Passing and crossing forbidden
 A10 Passage forbidden outside marked space

 A5 Forbidden to remain in area indicated
 A6 Anchoring forbidden
 A7 Mooring forbidden
 A8 Turning forbidden
 A9 Forbidden to create wash

Obligation signals

 B1 Take direction of arrow
 B2a Turn towards side of channel indicated
 B2b Turn towards side of channel indicates
 B3a Stay on side of channel indicated
 B3b Stay on side of channel indicated
 B4a Turn towards side of channel indicated
 B4b Turn towards side of channel indicated

 B5 Obligation to stop in certain circumstances
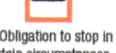 B6 Maximum speed allowed km/h
 B7 Sound your horn
 B8 Be especially carreful

Recommandation signals

 D1a Passage allowed from both directions
 D1b Passage allowed for your forbidden from the order side (one way only)
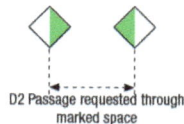 D2 Passage requested through marked space
 D3 Direction recommended

Restriction signals

 C1 Depth limited
 C2 Height above water level limited
 C3 Width limited
 C4 Special limitations
 C5 Channel is situated at distance indicated from bank

Rules of the Road and CEVNI

The **Indication Signals** inform the boater of objects, activities and things that are present or permissible along the next section, while the **Prohibition Signals** indicate activities that are not allowed along the next stretch. The **Obligation Signals** inform of actions that must be done, while the **Recommendation Signals** are less forceful and more suggestive, but they should be followed unless you have good reason not to. The **Restriction Signals** pertain to limitations of height, depth or width of the channel.

Most of these signals are clear and self-explanatory, so they are easy to decipher. Don't worry if you haven't memorized them all by the time you step aboard. Your rental boat will have a convenient card or a booklet that includes these signals and you can refer to it as you cruise.

In addition to the signs, there are the red and green traffic lights at many locks and mobile bridges. These are generally in a triangular pattern with two red lights vertically along the left side and a green in the lower right corner. If the two red lights are lit, the lock or bridge is out of service. If one red is lit you are being told to wait. If a red and a green are lit, the lock or bridge is being prepared for you and when the green alone is lit, you may proceed.

Besides the lights and the signs, CEVNI also regulates sound signals. These are used to signal your intentions and actions to other boaters and you should know the most common ones:

Horn signals

▬	•	••	•••	••••	••••••••
Attention (4 seconds)	I am coming towards starboard (1 second)	I am coming towards port	I am going into reverse	I am out of control	Danger of collision

The most common one is **Attention**, which is a long blast of about four seconds. This is the sound signal that is given when you see a **Sound Your Horn** sign, normally before a blind narrow bend, a one-way tunnel or other restricted passage. If you hear a long blast in such a place, sound one in return to indicate your presence, then apply the down-bound priority rule.

Increasingly complex sound signals are also used to signal other intended actions, including requests to overtake another vessel. However, since as a rental boat on small canals it is bad form for you to initiate an overtaking, you needn't know the details. Suffice it to say that if you hear two long blasts followed by one or two shorts from a barge astern, immediately it is safe to do so, slow down, pull over and let it pass.

For rivers and broad waterways, such as lakes, CEVNI has a system of buoys, beacons and other markers that vary from those found in coastal waters, but sufficiently based on them as to make them readily understood by those familiar with the COLREGs and IALA bouyage systems. If you are venturing from the confined and comparatively still waters of the canals and out onto a free-flowing river, then you must familiarize yourself with the basic system.

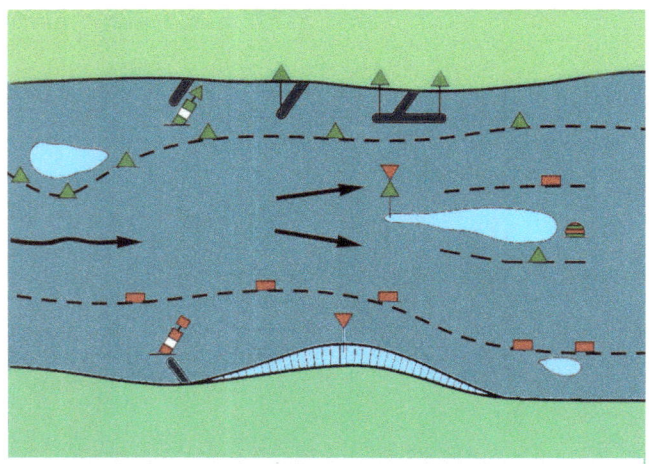

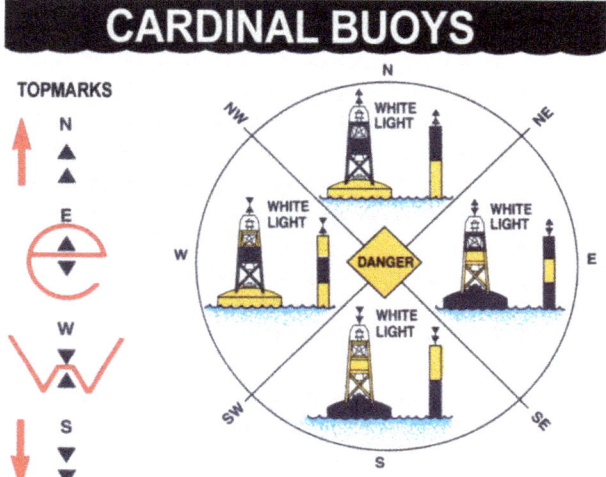

This diagram showing various uses of port-hand and starboard-hand buoys and beacons, plus bifurcation marks, indicates some of the uses of these aids to navigation. Without a firm grasp of their meaning, a boater will soon be aground on a mid-channel shoal, isolated shallow patches or foul ground near the river bank. In European waters, the buoyage follows the IALA Region A system, which is opposite to that used in North and South America. In Europe, when heading upstream, the red buoys are left to Port and the green are left to Starboard. The buoy colours match the colours of the navigational lights. Another way to remember this is: the **R**ight bank marks are **R**ed when **R**unning with the current downstream.

The main navigation marks to be familiar with are the lateral buoys and beacons. In addition to these are the cardinal buoys and beacons, which will guide you in safe direction from a hazard. These are much less commonly found inland than they are in coastal waters, but there are some on Étang de Thau near Sète in the Midi. These navigational marks indicate the direction toward safe water from the hazard. Aboard your boat will be a card or booklet showing the navigational marks that you are likely to encounter along the way.

Chapter Eleven

Lock Etiquette and Food for Thought

The aim of the following few paragraphs is to give a flavour of what to expect while cruising on the inland waterways of France.

If you are on a canal with manned locks, at your final lock each day the lock keeper will likely ask you if you intend continuing along the canal the next day, and if so, at what time. This is done so that lock staff can be organized and your movements are coordinated with other canal traffic. Also, it often means that the next locks can prepared for your passage. Keep to the timing that you arrange, otherwise it may foul-up the system, inconvenience the lock keepers and other boaters and ultimately delay yourself.

As you continue along the canal, inform the lock keeper if you plan to pause before the next lock, either to sightsee, to take a break or to stop for the day. This way, the next lock won't be held for you at the inconvenience of other boats and lock keepers. The lock keeper will ask you when you wish to continue so that your movement can be re-coordinated with lock staff and other boats.

If you plan on stopping for the day in a popular location, it makes good sense to arrive in the late morning or early in the afternoon, otherwise, all the mooring places might be occupied. If the place has a capitainerie or a marina office, you can phone ahead and reserve a space; the cruising guides have the phone numbers listed.

Also listed and often described in the better cruising guides are places of interest along the canal or a short distance away from it. A short walk into town will often be rewarded with wonderful historic buildings to look at or to visit. Remember that settlement first happened along the trade routes, such as on navigable rivers and in the easily traversed passes. Many of the French canals follow these routes and pass through cities, towns and villages that date back many centuries. Sadly, in many of the small towns and villages, the businesses have been gradually closing-down, the trade going increasingly to the chain supermarkets and big-box stores, normally sited at a highway intersection a short distance outside town.

Having bicycles aboard makes a lot of sense, not only to access these supermarkets, but also to explore the towns and villages that are beyond a reasonable walk from the canal. Additionally, some of the crew might enjoy bicycling along the canal towpath between locks, seeing the system from a different perspective. Bicycles are one of the options offered by the rental companies.

In the morning, while one person puts the coffee on, another heads off to the boulangerie for a fresh baguette or some butter croissants or possibly both. One of the most dependable things in France is that there will be a bakery nearby. Another dependable thing is that it will be closed one day mid-week, so the day before check if it will be open the next day. Another dependable thing in France is that bakeries will normally be closed from 1230 until mid-to-late afternoon, so if you plan on fresh-baked items for lunch, it is best to buy these in the morning on the breakfast run.

Many of the towns hold a street market one or more days each week. Local and regional farm produce and artisan items can be found at these, as well as a broad variety of other merchandise often offered by travelling merchants who rotate through the towns in the region. Market days and their locations are listed in some of the cruising guides. There is likely also a list of these on your boat, supplied by the rental base.

The guides also list the better or more popular restaurants within easy access of the canal. In July 2014 a new regulation was introduced in France to inform diners if menu items offered by a restaurant are industrially produced off-site or whether they are 'fait maison', homemade. This is great if you wish to dine on the famous French cuisine, rather than on a combination of canned, packaged, or pre-cooked items, soups and sauces from powder and other formula short-cuts. All French restaurants must now put the following key phrase on their menus and cartes: "Les plats 'fait maison' sont élaborés sur place à partir de produits bruts", which translates to "'Homemade dishes' are made on site from raw produce".

Restaurants that make everything from scratch must display the words 'fait maison' or the approved logo in a visible place, those restaurants that have a mix of homemade and industrial must put 'fait maison' next to every homemade menu item. Those restaurants that have no homemade dishes must still put the key phrase on their menus and cartes to remind diners of the regulation. In a survey conducted in 2014, nearly three-quarters of all French dining establishments serve industrially produced food, including some chic bistros and up-scale restaurants.

Lock Etiquette and Food for Thought

An option to searching for a restaurant is cooking and dining aboard. The galleys in most of the rental boats are equipped to allow more than just basic cooking. The French markets and supermarkets have wonderful ingredients that can be turned into gourmet feasts. Like the restaurants, you can choose to open packages, cans and bags, or you can buy fresh ingredients and make it from scratch. The wineries along the way have wines to taste, to select and to buy and the wine shops and supermarkets have a wide selections at realistic prices. For years our preferred option has been to dine aboard.

Your days along the canal can be as varied as your interests dictate. For those with inquisitive minds and an exploratory spirit, there will be no shortage of things to see and do along the way. You can move along at snail's pace taking days to go a few kilometres while thoroughly experiencing a small area, or you can move at a quicker pace through a much larger area to gain a broader perspective of the region. You can chose a boat with basic amenities and enjoy a more rustic adventure or you can go grand luxe in a boat with air-conditioning, a dish washer and large areas to relax. The choice of cruising style is yours just as is the choice of cruising region.

However you choose to do it, come, join us on the French canals.

Glossary of English and French Canal Terms

Accostable - French for an area where securing alongside is possible.

Accostage - French for a mooring, a place for watercraft to secure alongside. See also amarrage.

Accoster - French for the act of securing alongside. See also amarrer.

Air Draft - The height from waterline to the highest fixed structure of a watercraft. This is important to determine whether it will fit under a bridge or other structure across a waterway. Tirant d'aire in French.

à la Dérive - French for drifting, moving only by the current. See also culer.

Amarrage - French for moorage or mooring, a place for watercraft to secure alongside or the act of securing alongside. Also used to refer to the fees paid for using the facility.

Amarrer - French for being secured alongside. See also accoster.

Apparaux - French term for the equipment required by regulations to be carried in a watercraft.

Appontement - Another term for estacade, French for wharf, a structure to facilitate securing alongside a river or canal bank, often mistakenly called a dock.

Aqueduct - A structure that carries a canal over a road, railway or other watercourse. Pont-canal in French.

Avalant - French term used to refer to watercraft descending a waterway, and important in considering Right-of-Way.

Avitailler - French for provisioning a watercraft with all necessities for its operation and the support of its crew.

Bâbord - French for port, the left side of a watercraft or a direction to the left.

Bakery - A vital daily visit throughout France. Boulangerie in French.

Balise - French for beacon, a navigation stake or a pole in a waterway. See also fiche.

Barge - 1. A long, flat bottomed watercraft for carrying freight on canals and rivers. Many are now converted for pleasure use or live-aboard. Péniche in French. 2. A long ornamental watercraft used for pleasure or ceremony, as an Admiral's Barge, a Royal Barge or an elegant cruising yacht. Croisière or Vedette in French.

Barrage - French for weir, a low dam used to control the height and flow of water on a canalized river.

Bassinée - French for the maneuvers required to enter and exit a lock. Also sassée or éclusée.

Baulard - An alternate and seldom seen spelling of the French for bollard. See also bitte, bitte d'amarrage, bollard, boullard.

Beacon - A navigation stake or a pole in a waterway. Balise or fiche in French.

Beam - The width of the widest fixed structure of the hull of a watercraft. Largeur in French.

Glossary of English and French Canal Terms

Bec de chardonnet - French for the vertical hollow quoin or bearing in a lock wall to add to the watertight closure of the lock gate.

Berge - French for a river or canal embankment.

Bief - French for pound, the body of water between locks on a canal.

Bief de partage - French for summit pound, the body of water at the watershed of a canal marking the transition from ascending to descending locks.

Bitte or Bitte d'amarrage - French for bollard.

Bollard - French or English for a metal, masonry or wooden post or vertical structure around which lines are turned to secure or moor a watercraft. In locks, they can be fixed or floating. Baulard, bitte, bitte d'amarrage, bollard, boulard or pieu in French.

Bosse - French for a projection or promontory of the river bank.

Bouée - French for buoy, a floating navigation marker in a watercourse.

Boulangerie - French for bakery, a vital daily visit throughout France.

Boulard - An alternate spelling of the French for bollard. See also bitte, bitte d'amarrage, bollard, boullard, pieu.

Buoy - A floating navigation marker in a watercourse. Bouée in French.

Cajoler - French term meaning to swing in the current, as at anchor or on a mooring or when improperly secured alongside.

Cale à sèche - French for dry dock or dock. A chamber from which the water can be drained to facilitate work on a watercraft's bottom.

Capitainerie - French for the office of the marina manager.

Carburant - French for fuel.

Chamber - The area between the gates of a lock in which the water level changes to lift or lower a watercraft. Sas in French

Channel - The navigable route of a watercourse, usually the area of deepest water. Chenal in French.

Chemin de haulage - French for towpath, the path or roadway alongside a canal, formerly used for hauling a barge along by human or animal power. Now ideal for bicycling and walking.

Chenal - French for channel, the navigable route of a watercourse, usually the area of deepest water.

Chômage - French for stoppage, the temporary closing of part of a waterway for maintenance or repairs.

Cill - (also spelled Sill) The masonry shelf on which the upstream lock gates are mounted. Care must be taken to have the stern clear of it to prevent damage to the boat when descending. Faux busc and Mur de chute in French

Coche de plaisance - The VNF name applied to a pleasure boat of less than 15 meters length.

Coque - French for hull.

Crane or Gantry - A lifting machine. Grue or Portique in French

Croisière - French for cruiser or cruising yacht. Kruiser in Dutch.

Culer - French for drifting, moving only by the current. Also referred to as à la dérive.

Défense (en caoutchouc) - French for (rubber) fender. A cushion to absorb the berthing energy or to protect the hull from damage. May be fixed to a dolphin, wharf, quayside or hull, or temporarily suspended overboard.

Dérives Latérals - Broad paddles or leeboards fitted to the sides of shallow draft Dutch sailing barges. They are lowered to act as a stabilizing keel to counter the press of the wind. Swards in Dutch

Dérivation - French for diversion canal, usually a cut to bypass a winding or sharply bent section of a river.

Déversoir - French for overflow channel, a drain to divert water to a lower level and prevent flooding the banks of a waterway.

Digue - French for dike, usually an earthen structure alongside canals and rivers to maintain water within the watercourse.

Digue submergée - French for submerged dike, a structure submerged in the watercourse to control water flow.

Dike - Usually an earthen structure alongside canals and rivers to maintain water within the watercourse. Sometimes submerged in the watercourse to control water flow. Digue in French.

Dock - Another term for dry dock, a chamber from which the water can be drained to facilitate work on a watercraft's bottom. Often incorrectly used to refer to a moorage, jetty, float or wharf. Cale à sèche in French.

Dolphins - Vertical mooring posts, usually several in a line and often used as waiting places before locks on rivers. Ducs d'Albe in French.

Dry Dock - Another term for dock, a chamber from which the water can be drained to facilitate work on a watercraft's bottom. Often incorrectly used to refer to a moorage, jetty, float or wharf. Cale à sèche in French.

Draft - The depth of the lowest part of the watercraft below water. This is important to know to determine whether it can safely navigate a particular waterway. Tirant d'eau in French.

Ducs d'Albe - French for dolphins, vertical mooring posts, usually several in a line and often used as waiting places before locks on rivers.

Écluse - French for lock, a floodable chamber used to lift or lower watercraft on a canal or river.

Éclusée - French for the maneuvers required to enter and exit a lock. Also sassée or bassinée.

Éclusier - French for lock keeper.

Embranchement - French for a branch or an arm off the main canal.

Épicerie - Grocery store.

Escale - French for a short-term mooring for passenger vessels.

Estacade - French for wharf, a structure to facilitate securing to a river or canal bank, often

Glossary of English and French Canal Terms

mistakenly called a dock. See also appontement.

Fascines - French for brushwood faggots used to protect works such as bridge piers, jetties or embankments from current erosion.

Faux busc - French the upstream cill or sill, the masonry shelf on which the upstream lock gates are mounted. Care must be taken to have the stern clear of it to prevent damage to the boat when descending. Also mur de chute

Fender - A protective pad or buffer used to protect a watercraft or mooring from damage. Traditionally made of rope, but now usually made of plastic or rubber. Défense (en caoutchouc) in French.

Fiche - French for beacon, a navigation stake or a pole in a waterway. See also Balise.

Flood Gate - Gates along a navigation that are normally open except during floods. Porte de garde in French.

Franc bord - French for freeboard, the height of the lowest part of the deck of a watercraft above its waterline. See also revanche.

Freeboard - The height of the lowest part of the deck of a watercraft above its waterline. Franc bord or revanche in French.

Freycinet - The name given to the dimensions to which most French canals were standardized in 1877 to 1879. Named after Charles Louis de Saulces de Freycinet, the Minister of Public Works who was responsible for inland navigation, a Freycinet lock measures 39 metres by 5.20 metres and allows barges with a length of up to 38.5 metres, a beam of 5.05 metres and a draft of 1.80 metres to navigate.

Fuel - Carburant in French

Gabarit - French term for the maximum size of watercraft a particular waterway will allow to safely navigate.

Gaff - A long pole with a hook and a blunt spike on one end to assist in mooring or retrieving objects in the water. Gaffe in French.

Gaffe - French for gaff, a long pole with a hook and a blunt spike on one end to assist in mooring or retrieving objects in the water.

Ganche - French for the concave or outer curve formed by a river bank in a bend.

Gantry or Crane - A lifting machine. Portique or Grue in French

Gardiennage - French for moorage, the provision of a place for a watercraft to secure to land. Also used to refer to the fees paid for using a moorage facility. See amarrage.

Gasoil - French for diesel oil.

Gate - A movable door at each end of a lock chamber to hold back water and allow the changing of water levels. Vantail in French.

Gaz - French for propane or butane.

Gouvernail - French for rudder.

Grocery Store - Épicerie in French

Ground Paddle - A below ground valve or sluice that allows water into or out of a lock chamber.

Grue or Portique - A lifting machine, a crane or gantry.

Halte nautique - French for a simple mooring facility alongside the river or canal bank, with room for up to 30 pleasure craft. Water and garbage facilities and sometimes with electrical connections.

Haut fond - French for shoal, literally high bottom.

Hélice - French for propeller.

Hivernage - French for winterizing.

Largeur - French for width or beam, the width of the widest fixed structure of the hull of a watercraft.

Leeboards - Broad paddles fitted to the sides of shallow draft Dutch sailing barges. They are lowered to act as a stabilizing keel to counter the press of the wind. Dérives Latérals in French, Swards in Dutch.

Left Bank - The left side of a French waterway when facing downstream. Rive gauche in French.

Length (Overall) - The extreme length of a watercraft, including all fixed parts such as pulpits, rails, davits, swim platforms, etc. Longueur hors-tout in French. This is the measurement you need to determine whether the watercraft will fit in a lock or moorage.

Length (Registered) - The length measured from the foremost part of the main deck to the rearmost, but excluding any bow or stern projections, such as pulpits, guardrails, davits, swim platforms, etc. Longueur in French. This is the measurement on which license fees and if you are lucky, moorage fees are based.

Linguet - French for a short breakwater separating the immediate upstream approach to a lock from an adjacent weir to reduce the risk of being drawn toward the weir.

Lock - A floodable chamber used to lift or lower watercraft on a canal or river. Écluse in French.

Longueur - French for length. For registry purposes, this is measured from the fore most part of the main deck to the rearmost, but excluding any bow or stern projections, such as pulpits, guard rails, davits, swim platforms, etc.

Longueur hors-tout - French for overall length. The extreme length of a watercraft, including all fixed parts such as pulpits, rails, davits, swim platforms, etc. This is the measurement you need to determine whether the watercraft will fit in a lock or moorage.

Lourd (Bief lourd) - French for a reach of a river where the current is particularly strong.

Mediterranean Moorage - A space-saving method of securing a watercraft by dropping an anchor forward and backing to a wharf or embankment and making the stern fast with lines ashore.

Montant - French term used to refer to a watercraft ascending a waterway, and important in considering Right-of-Way.

Moorage - A place for a watercraft to secure to land or the act of securing with lines ashore. A float or buoy secured to the bottom of a body of water and to which a watercraft can secure away from land. Also used to refer to the fees paid for using a moorage facility. Amarrage in French.

Glossary of English and French Canal Terms

Mooring - A place for a watercraft to secure to land or the act of securing with lines ashore. A float or buoy secured to the bottom of a body of water and to which a ship can secure away from land. Amarrage in French.

Mooring Pins - Spikes or pins driven into the ground on the bank of a canal or river when no bollards are available for securing alongside.

Mur de chute - French for the height of the upstream cill or sill, the masonry shelf on which the upstream lock gates are mounted. Care must be taken to have the stern clear of it to prevent damage to the boat when descending. See also Faux busc.

NNN - French term for the guaranteed normal water level for navigation on a canal.

Paddle - A valve or sluice in a lock that allows water into or out of a lock chamber. Ventelle in French.

Passerelle - French for foot bridge.

PBEN, PHEC, PHEN - French terms for lowest navigable water level, highest water level known and highest navigable water level on rivers.

Percher - French term meaning to sound depths.

Péniche - French for barge. A long, flat bottomed watercraft for carrying freight on canal, river and estuaries. Many are now converted for pleasure use or live-aboard.

Pieu - French for bollard, a metal, masonry or wooden post or vertical structure around which lines are turned to secure or moor a watercraft. In locks, they can be fixed or floating. See also baulard, bitte, bitte d'amarrage, bollard or boulard.

Plafond - French for canal bed.

Pompe eaux usées - French for waste water pump or pump-out station.

Pont-canal - French for Aqueduct, a structure that carries a canal over a road, railway or other watercourse.

Pont levant, Pont mobile - French for lift bridge or mobile bridge.

Ponton - French for pontoon. A floating mooring.

Port - The left side of a watercraft or a direction to the left. Bâbord in French.

Port de plaisance - French for a large marina with space for over 60 non-commercial watercraft to moor, and equipped with electrical connections, water and most other marine facilities.

Porte d'écluse - French for lock door. The movable dams that allow the watercraft to enter a lock, the water level to be changed and the watercraft to exit at the new water level.

Porte de garde - Flood Gates along a navigation that are normally open except during floods.

Portique or Grue - A lifting machine, a gantry or crane.

Poteau busqué - French for a vertical hardwood sealing strip (often oak) used to improve watertightness between two lock gates or between a gate and the hollow quoin in the lock wall.

Poubelle - French for rubbish, garbage or gash disposal containers.

Pound - The body of water between locks of a canal. Bief in French.

Pump-out Station - A place to pump holding tanks. Pompe eaux usées in French.

Canal Cruising in France

Quai - French for quay, a mooring facility along a river or canal bank.

Quay - A mooring facility along a river or canal bank. Quai in French.

Relais nautique - French for a mooring facility alongside the river or canal bank, with room for 30 to 60 pleasure craft. Water and garbage facilities and sometimes with electrical connections.

Renard - French for a fissure or small break in a canal bank through which water leaks.

Revanche - French for freeboard, the height of the lowest part of the deck of a watercraft above its waterline. See also Franc bord.

Right Bank - The right side of a French waterway when facing downstream. Rive droite in French.

Risberme - French for a slope covered with brushwood faggots (fascines) at the base of a bridge pier, jetty or other structure to protect it from erosion by the current.

Rive droite - French for right bank, the right side of a French waterway when facing downstream.

Rive gauche - French for left bank, the left side of a French waterway when facing downstream.

Sas - French for lock chamber, the area between the gates of a lock in which the water level changes to lift or lower a watercraft.

Sassée - French for the maneuvers required to enter and exit a lock. Also bassinée or éclusée

Secure Alongside - To make fast a watercraft beam-to on an embankment or shore side mooring facility or to another vessel using mooring lines. Colloquially, the terms tie-up or moor are often used. Amarrage in French.

Sill - (also spelled Cill) The masonry shelf on which the upstream lock gates are mounted. Care must be taken to have the stern clear of it to prevent damage to the boat when descending. Faux busc and Mur de chute in French

Sluice - Among other things, a valve or paddle in a lock that allows water into or out of a lock chamber. Ventelle in French.

Souterrain - French for tunnel. Generally on a canal dug through the summit of a pass in order to prevent excessive climbing.

Starboard - The right side of a ship or a direction to the right. Tribord in French.

Stoppage - The temporary closing of part of a waterway for maintenance or repairs. Chômage in French.

Submerged Dike - A structure submerged in the watercourse to control water flow. Digue submergée in French.

Summit Pound - The body of water at the watershed of a canal marking the transition from ascending to descending locks. Bief de partage in French.

Tide Lock - A lock between fresh and tidal water. Some may rise or fall depending on the state of the tide.

Tirant d'aire - French for air draft. The height from waterline to the highest fixed structure of a watercraft. This is important to determine whether it will fit under a bridge or other structure across a waterway.

Glossary of English and French Canal Terms

Tirant d'eau - French for draft. The depth of the lowest part of the watercraft below water. This is important to know to determine whether it can safely navigate a particular waterway.

Towpath - The path or roadway alongside a canal, formerly used for hauling a barge along by human or animal power. Now ideal for bicycling and walking. Chemin de haulage in French.

Tribord - French for starboard, the right side of a watercraft or a direction to the right.

Tunnel - Generally on a canal dug through the summit of a pass in order to prevent excessive climbing. Souterrain in French.

Vantail - French for a lock gate.

Vedette - French for cruiser or cruising yacht. Kruiser in Dutch.

Ventelle - French for a paddle or sluice in a lock gate that allows water into or out of a lock chamber.

VNF - Voies Navigables de France - The French inland waterways authority that is responsible for the operation, maintenance and regulation of most of the French navigable rivers and canals.

Vignette - French term for the permit issued for a fee by the VNF for navigation on its waters.

Waste Water Pump-out - A place to pump holding tanks. Pompe eaux usées in French.

Weir - A low dam used to control the height and flow of water on a canalized river. Barrage in French.

Wharf - A structure to facilitate securing alongside a river or canal bank, often mistakenly called a dock. Appontement or estacade in French.

Lined-up for the entrance to an oval lock in the Midi

Then a simple engine move to bring the stern alongside

www.ingramcontent.com/pod-product-compliance
Lightning Source LLC
Chambersburg PA
CBHW061813290426
44110CB00026B/2863